THE FILMMAKER'S EYE

THE FILMMAKER'S EYE

LEARNING (AND BREAKING) THE RULES OF CINEMATIC COMPOSITION

GUSTAVO MERCADO

Focal Press
Taylor & Francis Group

NEW YORK AND LONDON

Front cover image: *Trois Couleurs: Blue* (Krzysztof Kieslowski, 1993). Courtesy of the Kobal Collection.

First published 2013 by Focal Press
70 Blanchard Road, Suite 402, Burlington, MA 01803

Simultaneously published in the UK by Focal Press
2 Park Square, Milton Park, Abingdon, Oxon OX14 4RN

Focal Press is an imprint of the Taylor & Francis Group, an informa business

Library of Congress Cataloging-in-Publication Data
Application submitted

ISBN 13: 978-0-240-81217-5 (pbk)

this book is dedicated to my parents, Julio and Maria Mercado, whose love and respect for film continues to inspire me.

contents

*Steadicam® is a registered trademark of the Tiffen Company

acknowledgments

I would like to express my gratitude to all the individuals who helped in the preparation of this book through their kind support, contributions, and expertise.

I am sincerely grateful to the team at Focal Press: Robert Clements, Anne McGee, Dennis Schaefer, Chris Simpson, and especially Elinor Actipis, who provided me with invaluable guidance and suggestions from start to finish (including a great title), took the time to nurture a first time author, and had an unwavering commitment to preserving the original concept behind this book.

I also want to thank my colleagues in the Film & Media Studies Department at Hunter College of the City University of New York, whose passion and dedication to studying and teaching the art and craft of film has always been a source of encouragement and inspiration, among them: Richard Barsam, Michael Gitlin, Andrew Lund, Ivone Margulies, Joe McElhaney, Robert Stanley, Renato Tonelli, Shanti Thakur, and Joel Zuker. I also want to acknowledge the support of Hunter College President Jennifer J. Raab, Provost Vita C. Rabinowitz, Dean Shirley Clay Scott, and Film & Media Studies Department Chair James Roman, who foster an atmosphere that encourages faculty scholarship and excellence in teaching.

I am also grateful to Jerry Carlson, David Davidson, Herman Lew, and Lana Lin at the City College of the City University of New York, who were generous with their knowledge and mentorship, and to Elvis Maynard for his research assistance.

My reviewers provided me with wonderful suggestions and undoubtedly made this a better book than it would have been: David A. Anselmi at the University of California Berkeley Extension, David Crossman at Ravensbourne College of Design and Communication, David Tainer at DePaul University, and especially Katherine Hurbis-Cherrier at New York University, who always had *le mot juste* whenever I needed it.

Special thanks go to my sweet wife Yuki Takeshima, who was endlessly patient, supportive, and understanding through many late nights of writing, and unconditionally sacrificed a lot of her time so that I could stare at a monitor day after day.

But I am most grateful of all to my teacher, colleague, mentor, and friend, Mick Hurbis-Cherrier, whose tireless and illuminating comments, assistance, ideas, and guidance were instrumental in the development of the manuscript. His teachings and passion for cinema resonate through every page of the book you now hold in your hands.

Up in the Air. *Jason Reitman, 2009.*

introduction

A group of friends and I went to see Jason Reitman's *Up in the Air* (2009) soon after it was released. Returning from the theatre, we discussed the movie; some of my friends liked it, some found it a bit slow, and others thought it was a masterpiece. At one point, the discussion focused on the cinematography, and one of my friends recalled how brilliant the shot shown on the opposite page was. Regardless of our opinions on the film, we all agreed with him about how beautiful and meaningful that shot had been. Interestingly, we could recall everything about this shot clearly: its composition, when it had happened in the film, and most importantly why it was such a great shot. While there were many other interesting shots and moments in the film, there was something particularly special about this shot that really resonated with all of us, regardless of how we felt about the film as a whole. What was it? Was it the composition of the shot? The acting? Or was there something else that made this shot so memorable?

To understand why this shot works so well, we need to know a bit about the context in which it appears. Natalie (Anna Kendrick), is a corporate up and comer who devises a way to fire employees remotely using webcams, saving her company (a professional corporate termination service) a lot of money spent flying their specialists to companies who need their services. Ryan (George Clooney), a senior firing specialist who is dubious of a system that precludes all real human contact, questions its soundness. Their boss promptly puts Ryan in charge of Natalie's education, and the two are sent out as a team, so Natalie can experience firsthand firing someone face to face. After a heart-wrenching montage of employees reacting to the news of their firing, the film cuts to a shot of Natalie sitting alone in a room full of empty of-fice chairs as she waits for Ryan. When he arrives to pick her up he asks her if she is OK, but she shrugs off the question, and they leave together. Now that we know the backstory of the shot, we can better understand what makes it work so well. In terms of its composition, the shot does not appear to be particularly complex. It looks like a simple wide shot of Natalie surrounded by empty office chairs. If we look closer, however, and break down the shot into its visual elements, the rules of composition used to arrange them in the frame, and its technical aspects, a more complex picture emerges, literally.

The use of a long shot (a shot that includes a subject's entire body and a large portion of their surrounding area) allowed the inclusion of a lot of chairs clustered around Natalie, emphasizing the large number of people she fired on that day, and makes her look small and lonely in the frame. The slight high angle also creates a composition that makes the empty chairs easy to see; if the shot had been taken at her eye level, for instance, most of the chairs would have been blocked from sight by the ones in the foreground. The high angle also makes Natalie look defeated, vulnerable, and distraught (high angles are often used to convey these emotions in characters). Natalie's placement in the frame follows the rule of thirds, creating a dynamic composition that gives her viewing room on the side of the frame she is facing; more importantly, this placement also makes it look as if the chairs were pushing her into a corner, physically and emotionally (placing her at the center of the composition would not have conveyed this idea). The camera to subject distance/aperture combination resulted in a shot with a deep depth of field, preventing us from concentrating our attention solely on her and ensuring that the chairs are as significant to our understand of this shot as she is (the filmmaker could have used a shallow depth of field, isolating her in the composition). All of these compositional decisions convey a very specific idea regarding how Natalie really feels at that moment, regardless of what she tells Ryan when he picks her up. The composition of this shot tells the audience that behind the corporate, no-nonsense exterior she projects, she hides an emotional side of her personality, one that is affected by the real human fallout of her profession. But the beauty and dramatic weight of this shot is not the result of simply applying the rules of composition; this shot works as well as it does because its technical elements, compositional choices, and narrative context, all work in concert to create meaning. The shot made a strong and lasting impression on my friends and me because it was not just visually striking, but more importantly, narratively resonant and eloquent.

This book presents an integrated approach to understanding and applying the rules of cinematic composition, one that takes into account the technical and narrative aspects that make shots like the example from *Up in the Air* so powerful. This new approach provides a deep and discursive exploration into one of the fundamental elements of the visual language of cinema- the shot. By focusing on the rules of cinematic composition as they apply to each of the most widely used shots of the cinematic vocabulary, examining the tools and know-how necessary to create them, and analyzing each shot's narrative function within their respective films, a clearer picture emerges about what it takes to create images that are visually compelling and narratively meaningful. But why focus on the rules of composition as they apply to specific shot types instead of looking at these principles in a broader, more general sense, as they can be applied to any visual composition? The answer is simple. As the language of cinema developed, certain rules of composition have become standardized in the way they are applied to certain shots, just like some technical conventions (regarding the use of lenses and depth of field, for instance) are more commonly found in certain shots and not others. These technical and visual conventions are intricately connected to narrative conventions, which over time have linked key moments in a story with the use of particular shots. A detailed analysis of how these visual, technical, and narrative conventions apply to each specific shot type can reveal the mechanics that contributed to their becoming conventions in the first place.

Another concept this book proposes is that the rules of cinematic composition are not written in stone. The so-called rules are remarkably flexible and can be subverted when appropriate, creating shots that have a fresh impact and resonate in surprising or even contradictory ways. For this reason, every shot analyzed includes an example where the rules were broken, yet made to work in creative, unexpected, and narratively compelling ways. You will find that the old adage "learn the rules so you know how to break them properly" works just as advertised.

The integrated approach of this book and its specific focus on the basic building blocks of the cinematic vocabulary preclude a comprehensive discussion of every possible concept and technical aspect related to visual composition. However, you will find a number of essential terms related to composition and cinematography in bold in most chapters. These frequently used terms are defined in the *Principles of Composition and Technical Concepts* chapter. If you wish to develop a more encyclopedic understanding of every concept and rule however, you should consider other sources that deal with visual composition as a comprehensive subject. I highly recommend Bruce Block's *The Visual Story: Creating the Visual Structure of Film, TV, and Digital Media*, also published by this press; it is a well illustrated, insightful look at visual composition that covers both basic and advanced components. For a solid guide to the technical aspects of film and video production, I recommend a book I was lucky to work on as an illustrator, written by my friend, mentor, and colleague Mick Hurbis-Cherrier, titled *Voice & Vision: A Creative Approach to Narrative Film and DV Production*, also published by this press. In many ways, *The Filmmaker's Eye* was inspired by the integrated approach *Voice & Vision* uses to cover every technical, aesthetic, narrative, and logistical aspect of film and video preproduction, production, and post-production to develop the creative vision of the filmmaker.

  The Filmmaker's Eye takes a new approach to understanding the rules of cinematic composition (and how to break them) and to using them to move beyond basic utilitarian narrative conventions. This is most definitely not a "paint by the numbers" approach to cinematic composition; you should not be subservient to the dictates of a technique, but make the technique work for the specific needs of your story instead. The aim is to make you aware of the tonal impact and thematic resonance that is possible with a more complete understanding of the role each shot plays in the larger narrative and thematic scheme of your story. This comprehensive and integrated conceptualization of every shot in your film is essential to truly harness the power of this art form and connect with the audience. I hope the chapters in this book will inspire you to think about your shots in this more dynamic way the next time you set up the camera and get ready to frame your next shot. Good luck.

The Godfather. *Francis Ford Coppola, 1978.*

finding the frame

I recently had the opportunity to attend the screening of a short film by a beginning filmmaker. The first scene started with a shot of a young couple sitting on a couch, having an increasingly heated argument. The shot was wide enough to include most of the room, which was littered with magazines, DVDs, empty beer cans, a collection of sneakers stashed under the couch, and movie posters on every wall (obviously the young director's place). A small table could also be seen in the foreground of the shot, with a game console and a stack of video games prominently displayed on it. After the film ended, there was a Q & A session with the director, who looked very proud of his work and eager to answer questions. A man in the audience asked: "Was the guy on the couch trying to act like Travis Bickle?" The filmmaker look puzzled, and asked him why he was asking about Travis Bickle. The man answered he thought the large *Taxi Driver* poster right behind the actor was part of the story. "No, that poster just happened to be there," the filmmaker replied. Another audience member asked: "Was he trying to scam money from her to buy more video games?" The director look confused. "Was she upset with him because he doesn't clean up?" someone else asked. The filmmaker, obviously frustrated by now, stopped the Q & A to explain that the scene in question was really about the young couple trying to avoid having their first argument since they had just gotten married, and that he thought this should have been obvious by the way the young man's hand was nervously twitching as he held his wife's hand. The movie posters, video games, and the messy room were not really meant to be important parts of the scene and the story. The director was, however, pleased when someone asked him if a shot from the end of his film, where the couple was shown walking towards the camera in slow-motion, was an homage to a similar shot from Quentin Tarantino's *Reservoir Dogs* (1992). "Yes!" he replied. "I'm glad you caught that." When asked about the significance of that reference to his story, he answered: "I thought it'd look cool," to a still puzzled audience. The rest of his film had the same issues the opening shot and his homage shot had; there was a complete disconnection between the composition of his shots and their function within the narrative of his film.

The biggest mistake this director made was failing to create compositions that reflected meaningful aspects of his story. In the opening scene, he framed a shot that was visually dense, filled with details that turned out to be extraneous to the story and prevented the audience from getting the point he was trying to make. By prominently including the movie posters, the game console, the sneakers under the couch, and the empty beer cans, the twitching hand of the husband was lost in the shot; the audience was unable to glean the intended meaning of the composition. When the director watched the shot through the viewfinder of the camera during production, he did not notice anything else besides the twitching hand of the husband in the frame, because he already knew that was a meaningful detail in the scene; his audience did not. In the last shot of his film, the director was able to duplicate a composition he had seen in another film, and although the shot briefly elicited a positive response from the audience, it later became a source of confusion when they realized that it had no meaningful connection with the story. The director simply did not think about his story in a cinematic way, to create shot compositions that visually emphasized significant plot details of his story as well as its themes, motifs, and core ideas. If he had understood the relationship between the technical aspects of filmmaking, the narrative function each type of shot can have, and the rules of composition, his audience's reaction to his film would have been vastly different.

If you want to become an effective storyteller, one of the most important things you can do is to have a clear vision of your story, so that it reflects your unique take on it, not somebody else's. You already do this without thinking whenever you share an anecdote about something that happened to you. Let us say, for instance, that you want to let a friend know about the time someone got upset when you accidentally cut them off while driving and they chased you down the highway. You would not begin your story by describing what you did on that day as soon as you woke up, how long it took you to take a shower, the articles you read on a blog while having breakfast, the clothes you were wearing, or any other meaningless detail that occurred before you got into your car and drove down the highway. Intuitively, you would edit your story to include only the most important parts, so that your friend would understand how terrifying/interesting/crazy your road rage encounter really was. The director of the short film did not do this when he shot his film. By leaving all those unnecessary details in the composition of his shots, he did the equivalent of describing the color of the socks the guy sitting on the couch was wearing, instead of showing his audience how uncomfortable and nervous the husband was feeling while holding the hand of his wife.

Anything and everything that is included in the composition of a shot will be interpreted by an audience as being there for a specific purpose that is directly related and necessary to understand the story they are watching. This is one of those conventions that has been developed over thousands of years of visual storytelling (even cavemen knew not to include extraneous details in cave paintings!), and continues to be as important today as the first day it was used. If we take this principle just a bit further, we could add that the placement, size, and visibility of anything in the frame will also affect how an audience understands its importance to the story.

Take a look at the shot from Francis Ford Coppola's *The Godfather* (1972) at the beginning of this chapter. It is an extreme long shot that shows a car parked on a deserted road, with someone in the backseat pointing a gun at someone sitting in the front seat. In the distant background, the Statue of Liberty is visible above a bank of wild grass. This seemingly simple composition has a very clear meaning: someone is being murdered inside a car on a deserted road. In fact, this shot's meaning is so clear that even someone who has never seen *The Godfather* would have no trouble understanding what is happening at this moment in the story. This shot is an excellent example of including only what is absolutely necessary in the frame to get the point being conveyed by the director. If you have been paying attention and observed the shot closely, you should be curious about a little detail included in the composition of this shot. If everything in the frame is meant to be meaningful and necessary to understand the story, then why is the Statue of Liberty part of the composition of this shot? Is it there simply to establish the location of the murder? Why is it so distant and tiny in the frame? If you look at the shot carefully, you will notice that the statue is facing away from the car where the murder is taking place. Could this be a meaningful detail? If it is in the frame, then everything about it, from its placement to the angle from which it was shot, has to be meaningful.

Let us recount the example where you shared your road rage incident with a friend. When you told your story, you left out irrelevant details, describing the events from your unique point of view, since you experienced them firsthand. But what if the day of the incident happened to be the very first time you were driving on a highway? How do you think that would have changed the way you told the story? More importantly, do you think your friend would have felt differently about how meaningful this event was to you? You probably would have emphasized your lack of driving experience, and how this incident made you weary of driving on highways, or how particularly difficult it was to exit from the highway when you noticed the guy was following you. In other words, your unique experience (not only of the event itself, but also your life experience) would have prompted you to contextualize the event, emphasizing and adding details that would have inflected your story so that it reflected your individual experience of it. Creating meaningful compositions works in the same way; the framing of your shots should reflect your understanding of the story in a way that conveys your perspective, your values, your idiosyncrasies, your vision. When Coppola chose to include the Statue of Liberty in his shot from *The Godfather*, seen from that particular angle, at that particular size and placement in the frame, this is exactly what he was doing; he was adding his perspective to this event in the story, commenting on it, conveying much more than just the murder of a man inside a car. What do you think including such a recognizable symbol of freedom, the American Dream, and the immigrant journey says about the killing of the man in the car?

When the director of the short film used the same shot composition as the famous slow motion shot from the opening of *Reservoir Dogs*, he expected the audience to connect with his story in the same way they had connected with the Tarantino film. This was not the case, because the effectiveness of the original shot worked within the context of that story, and while the audience had a reaction when they recognized the homage he was making, the shot was eventually rendered meaningless once they realized it had absolutely nothing to do with the story they watched in his film. The composition of a shot conveys meaning not only through the arrangement of visual elements in a frame, but also by the context in which it is presented. A high angle shot (where the camera is placed so that it looks down on a subject), for instance, is commonly used when trying to convey that a character feels defeated, lacking in confidence, or psychologically vulnerable; while this is a common usage of this kind of shot, you cannot simply assume that your audience will automatically infer those connotations whenever you use this angle, unless the context in your story supports it. There has to be a direct connection between what takes place in the story and the use of a particular composition. This is exactly how certain visual conventions, like showing characters walking in slow motion towards the camera, became associated with certain connotations in the first place. Additionally, because so much of the meaning of a shot is derived by the context in which it is presented, it is possible to subvert the commonly associated connotations of certain shots. You could, for instance, use a high angle shot to convey that a character is confident, assertive, and in control, and nobody in the audience would find the composition ironic or ineffective, if the context in which you use it is supported within your story (see the chapter on the medium close up for an example of a high angle shot used in this way).

But how do you decide which story elements should be used to motivate your choice of shot size and composition? Which context should support your shot selection? Before you can make a decision about where to place the camera, you need to understand exactly what should dominate the composition, what should be included and excluded from it, and what meaning will be conveyed by the shot beyond what is contained in the frame. One strategy is to identify the themes and ideas that lie at the heart of your story, its essence, its core ideas. What is your story really about? Effective stories have strong core ideas that add emotional depth and context, allowing the audience to connect with what you are showing them. John G. Avildsen's *Rocky* (1976), for instance, tells the story of a small-time boxer who gets a one-in-a-million chance to fight for the heavyweight championship of the world. Only that is not what the story is really about. *Rocky* is really about a man who once had a lot of potential as a boxer but squandered it and never amounted to much, seeing himself as a failure because of it. Training for the heavyweight championship makes him realize that he can still have a chance to be somebody, to regain his self-respect and to be respected by others. Gaining self-respect: this is the core idea, the main thematic context behind the story of *Rocky*. Every decision behind the composition of every shot can now be designed to support this core idea, with a visual strategy (the set of decisions related to the use of stocks, color, lighting, lenses, depth of field, filtration, and color correction, among others) that reflects the theme of self-respect throughout the film. If the unfilmed script for *Rocky* landed on your desk and you were given a one-in-a-million chance to direct the film, how would you go about creating compositions that reflect the core idea of "regaining self-respect?"

You could, for instance, plot the journey Rocky takes toward self-respect, so that the scenes at the beginning of the film, while he is still unmotivated to change his ways, are shot from a slight high angle, making him look like he lacks confidence and feels psychologically vulnerable (the conventional use of a high angle shot, but used here within a well thought-out context and visual strategy). As Rocky trains harder and focuses on his goal, the camera could slowly switch to using slight low angle shots, subtly conveying his increasing confidence and change in attitude. This simple decision alone could be enough to create compositions that reflect your take on the story, but you could have combined it with any of the rules of composition shown in this book as well. You could, for instance, create a visual strategy where the placement of the character in the frame is also plotted throughout the film to match his journey toward self-respect, so that he is placed off-center, in consistently unbalanced compositions at the beginning of the film and in more balanced framings toward the end, or use wide angle lenses and then switch to telephotos, or start with shallow depths of field and then use deep depths of field, or use handheld shots at the beginning and static shots toward the end; you get the point.

Whatever visual strategy you decide to use based on the core ideas of your story should be used consistently throughout your film for your audience to understand its intended meaning within the context you created. This means that the compositional choices you make should work at every level of your film, starting with every single shot, then every scene, every sequence, and the entire film as a whole. If you use a particular shot composition to mean "he lacks confidence" at one point in your story, you should then avoid using the same shot composition to mean anything else other than "lacking confidence," or else the audience will fail to connect with the core ideas in your story even if they can follow the events that take place in it. Every shot counts, no matter how inconsequential it might seem (and no shot should be inconsequential in the first place since it is included in your film, right?).

Going back to the shot of the young couple sitting on the couch. What could the director have done differently? The right questions to ask really are: what is the core idea of his story? What about the core idea of that particular scene? What is this scene really about besides the couple trying to avoid having an argument? Based on the answers to these questions, the director could have devised a visual strategy to support the core ideas of his story; he could have then created compositions that supported them, using the rules of cinematic composition analyzed in this book. Following (or breaking, provided you do it within the proper context) the rules of cinematic composition can ensure that you create visually compelling images, but they can only truly connect with an audience when they express your vision of the story; this is the most important step you can take to develop your own visual style and voice as a filmmaker.

principles of composition
and technical concepts

aspect ratios

Every compositional decision you make will be first defined by the dimensions of your frame. The ratio between the width and height of the frame is referred to as the aspect ratio, and it differs depending on the shooting format. The most common aspect ratios are 2.39:1 (called anamorphic or scope, originally 2.35:1 until the 1970s), 1.85:1 (American theatrical standard, also called "flat"), 1.66:1 (European theatrical standard), 1.78:1 (the HDTV standard that is also called 16x9, used in HD cameras), and 1.33:1 (the aspect ratio of 16mm and 35mm shooting formats, and also the theatrical format used until the 1950s, and analog TV). It is essential to know both the aspect ratio of the shooting format and the exhibition/distribution format to ensure that the compositional choices you make as part of your visual strategy in production will be preserved.

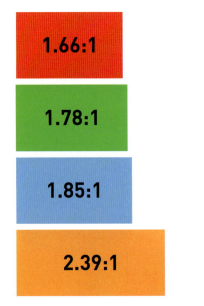

most common exhibition/distribution aspect ratios

frame axes

Since the frame is essentially two-dimensional, it is defined by two axes, a horizontal or x axis, and a vertical or y axis. A third axis that denotes the depth in a frame, or z axis, can be emphasized by the use of depth cues (examined later in this chapter), to create deep frames, or purposely understated, to create flat frames, as shown in the two examples below from Steve McQueen's *Hunger* (2008). Most often however, filmmakers tend to create compositions in depth, emphasizing the z axis to overcome the inherent flatness of the frame and enhance verisimilitude. Perceived distances and movement along each one of these axes can also be manipulated by the type of lens used, altering the visual relationship between subjects and the space around them.

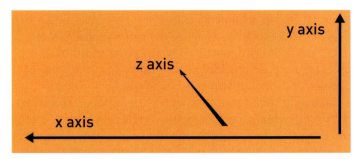

frame axes

a deep frame that emphasizes the z axis

a flat frame that understates the z axis

the rule of thirds

Some of the conventions used to create visually harmonious compositions have been developed over hundreds of years of artistic experimentation and development; one of the oldest is known as the rule of thirds. By dividing the frame into thirds along its width and height, sweet spots are created at their cross points, providing a guide for the placement of important compositional elements that results in dynamic compositions. The lines themselves are also often used as guides for the placement of horizons in extreme long shots and establishing shots. When subjects are placed in the frame according to the rule of thirds, it is common to position their eyes over one of these spots, the top left sweet spot if they are looking towards the right side of the frame, or the top right if they are looking at the left side of the frame, as seen in the example in the next column from Wong Kar Wai's *Fallen Angels* (1995). This placement ensures that they are given enough looking room, a convention designed to balance the composition by countering the compositional weight of the subject's gaze. If looking room is not added (for instance by placing the subject at the center of the frame while they are looking toward either side) the composition will feel static and lack visual tension, which in some cases might be exactly what you want to convey. The placement of a subject using the top line also gives them the proper

amount of headroom: the positioning of the subject's head in relation to the top of the frame. The amount of headroom is a function of the size of the subject in the frame, so that subjects in a close up should have their heads cropped by the top of the frame for proper headroom, while subjects in a long shot should have a sizable amount of headroom above their heads. The rule of thirds also applies to subject placement as they move across the x axis of the frame; if they are moving toward the right side, they should be placed along the left vertical line to give them proper walking room, and vice versa, unless you want to create a composition that purposely feels uneasy and unbalanced.

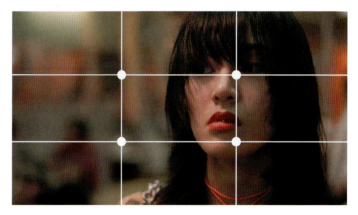

subject placement using the rule of thirds

Hitchcock's rule

An amazingly simple yet extremely effective principle that Alfred Hitchcock shared with François Truffaut during the writing of Truffaut's *Hitchcock/Truffaut*, states that the size of an object in the frame should be directly related to its importance in the story at that moment. This principle can be applied whether you have only one or several visual elements in the frame, and can be used to create tension and suspense, especially when the audience does not know the reason behind the visual emphasis being placed on the object or subject. In the example below, from Rob Reiner's *Misery* (1990), a tiny ceramic penguin is composed so that it fills the frame, since it will be the clue that later alerts Annie (Kathy Bates) that Paul Sheldon (James Caan), a writer she has imprisoned in her house, has in fact managed to leave his locked room.

Hitchcock's rule in action

balanced/unbalanced compositions

Every object included in a frame carries with it a visual weight. The size, color, brightness, and placement of an object can affect the audience's perception of its relative visual weight, making it possible to create compositions that feel balanced when the visual weight of the objects in the frame is evenly distributed, or unbalanced when the visual weight is concentrated in only one area of the frame. Although the terms balanced and unbalanced have no inherent value judgement in terms of composition, it is not uncommon to find balanced compositions that have their visual weight distributed symmetrically or evenly in the frame being used to convey order, uniformity, and predetermination. Likewise, unbalanced compositions are often associated with chaos, uneasiness,

and tension. Ultimately, the feeling that can be communicated by the use of balanced and unbalanced compositions will depend largely on the narrative context in which they are being used. In the example below, from Zhang Yimou's *Hero* (top, 2004), a balanced composition is used to convey that we are about to see a duel between equally-matched adversaries, adding suspense and tension to the scene. The placement of subjects in the example from John Hillcoat's *The Proposition* (bottom, 2005), also creates tension by framing them in an unbalanced composition as they witness the unjust punishment of a young man. Note that although the composition is unbalanced, with most of the visual weight on the bottom right corner of the frame, the main subject was still positioned according to the rule of thirds.

a balanced composition

an unbalanced composition

high and low angles

The height of the camera relative to a subject can be used to manipulate the audience's relationship to that subject. Eye-level shots place the camera at a height that matches the subject's eyes. A high angle shot places the camera above eye-level, and results in a framing that has the audience looking down on a subject. A low angle shot, on the other hand, places the camera below eye-level, and lets the audience look up at a subject. It is very common to see low angle shots used to convey confidence, power, and control, and high angle shots weakness, passiveness, and powerlessness, but these interpretations are not absolute and can be subverted based on the context in which they are presented. A common misuse of high and low angle shots is

low angle shot

high angle shot

to frame the subject at too steep an angle, which results in a very dynamic but at times distracting composition. Only a minor adjustment of the placement of the camera right below or above eye level is sufficient to make an impression in the minds of the audience. The two examples on the left, from Florian Henckel von Donnersmarck's *The Lives of Others* (2006), use this principle to convey two very different emotional states; the top frame uses a slight low angle that shows a confident and even menacing Wiesler (Ulrich Mühe), an officer for the Stasi, as he systematically and mercilessly interrogates a suspect until he makes him confess. The bottom frame, from much later in the film, uses a high angle that emphasizes the tension and fear he experiences as he monitors agents raiding the house of a dramatist he protects at great personal risk.

depth cues

Creating depth to overcome the inherent two-dimensionality of the frame is one of the most common compositional strategies designed to produce a dynamic frame and a believable three dimensional space. While there are several techniques to add depth to a composition, two of the most frequently used by filmmakers are the relative size and object overlapping depth cues. The relative size depth cue is based on our assumption that if two objects are of the same size, seeing a smaller one is perceived as it being farther away, creating the illusion of depth. Filmmakers exploit this technique by placing subjects along the z axis of the frame, as shown in the example on the next page from Quentin Tarantino's *Inglourious Basterds* (top, 2009). Object overlapping entails just what its name says: the overlapping of objects along the z axis. When an object is seen partially covering or overlapping another object, we perceive the covered object as being farther away from us, creating the illusion of depth in the composition. The use of this technique by filmmakers usually involves finding any excuse to place something in the foreground of the frame, partially blocking our view of the focal point of the composition. The O.T.S., or over the shoulder shot, is probably the most common example of this technique, but it is not uncommon to see filmmakers place objects in the foreground simply to add depth to the frame, as seen in Michael Bay's *The Rock* (bottom, 1996), where the chains in the foreground add depth and frame the subject (Nicolas Cage) within the frame, ensuring he is the focal point of the composition.

relative size depth cue

overlapping objects

closed frames and open frames

Closed frames refer to shots that do not acknowledge or require the existence of off-screen space to convey their narrative meaning, since all the information necessary for this purpose is contained within the edges of the frame. Open frames do not contain all the necessary information to understand their narrative meaning, and therefore require and draw attention to the existence of elements off-screen. Many compositional techniques are designed to imply the existence of off-screen space, since it acknowledges that the frame does not contain the entire world of the story, but instead acts like a window through which a larger world exists. However, there are benefits to using both of these types

a closed frame

an open frame

of frames depending on the needs of your story. Off-screen space is also exploited to create tension and suspense, particularly in the thriller and horror genres. In the two examples on the previous page, from Uli Edel's *The Baader Meinhof Complex* (2008), a closed frame (top) is used to emphasize the isolation Ulrike (Martina Gedeck), a member of a German terrorist organization, feels while serving time in jail. The open frame used in the second example adds tension to a shoot-out between Petra (Alexandra Maria Lara), another member of the organization, and the German police trying to apprehend her after she broke through a roadblock.

focal points

One way to ensure your compositions clearly convey the idea or concept you want to communicate is to use strong focal points. Focal points refer to the center of interest in a composition, the area where the viewer's gaze will gravitate to because of the arrangement of all the visual elements in the frame. Focal points can include one or several subjects, and are commonly created by using the rules of composition listed previously in this chapter, like the rule of thirds, Hitchcock's rule, and balanced/unbalanced compositions. In fact, you will notice that nearly all of the examples used in this book have very strong focal points. By carefully selecting what is included and excluded from the frame, what is in focus and out of focus, what is lit and unlit, and what visually dominates the frame, you can create compositions that will not be misunderstood by your audience; this is one of the most important principles to create eloquent, compelling images. The frame below, from Rolf de Heer's *Bad Boy Bubby* (1993), is a particularly good example of a composition with a very strong focal point, utilizing a visual trope (looking to the horizon as if to their future) that has been used by filmmakers as varied as George Lucas and Werner Herzog.

180° rule

This rule is designed to maintain the spatial continuity that should exist whenever subjects interact in a scene, and will therefore directly impact where they should be placed in the frame. Simply put, it states that the camera should always

following the 180° rule

a composition with a strong focal point

be placed on only one side of the imaginary line that is created by the looking or moving direction of the characters as established in wider shots. If the rule is not followed and the line is crossed, the resulting shots will not cut together properly, since subjects will not appear to be facing the right direction. In the examples on the previous page, from Terrence Malick's *The Thin Red Line* (1998), a conversation between Sgt. Welsh (Sean Penn) and Pvt. Witt (Jim Caviezel) places each camera angle on the same side of the 180° line, so that their looking direction remains consistent.

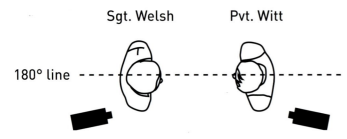

focal length

One way to classify lenses is according to their focal length, which equals the measurement, in millimeters, from the optical center (the point in the lens where the image is flipped and reversed) to the recording surface (a film frame or a CCD, or charge-coupled device, sensor in a video camera). Understanding focal length is important because it has a direct impact on the way lenses show perspective along the z axis, and on the field of view spanning the x axis. Lenses that reproduce perspective the way a human eye sees it are called normal; in the 16mm format, a normal lens has a focal length of 25mm, while in the 35mm format, a normal lens has a 50mm focal length. Any lens that has a focal length shorter than the normal for its format is referred to as a wide angle lens, while any lens with a focal length longer than the normal is called a telephoto lens.

field of view

Field of view refers to how much space along the x and y axis a lens can include in the frame. Lenses with short focal lengths (wide angles) have a greater field of view than lenses with long focal lengths (telephotos). Understanding this concept can let you include or exclude visual elements in your composition simply by choosing a lens based on focal length and its corresponding field of view.

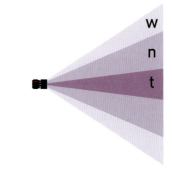

field of view of a wide (w), normal (n) and a telephoto lens (t)

wide angle lenses

Wide angle lenses capture a wider field of view than normal and telephoto lenses, and distort distances along the z axis, making them appear longer than they actually are. These lenses also exaggerate the perceived rate of movement along the z axis, so that if a subject approaches or moves away from the lens it will appear to do so much faster than normal. Wide angles produce the appearance of a deeper depth of field than normal or telephoto lenses, but if their focal length is too short (a feature of "fisheye" lenses) they can distort the edges of the frame, creating what is called a "barreling" effect. Wide angle lenses are not commonly used too close to a subject, because of the distortion they can add to faces, as seen in the example on the next column, from Wong Kar Wai's *Fallen Angels* (1995).

wide angle lens distortion

normal lenses

Normal lenses reproduce perspective in a way that closely resembles what a person would see if he or she stood where the camera is, except for the field of view, which is much greater in human eyesight thanks to our peripheral vision. Normal lenses are commonly used for shooting human subjects, especially close ups, since they do not distort faces like wide angle or telephoto lenses do. Distances and movement along the z axis of the frame are not exaggerated with normal lenses.

telephoto lenses

Long focal length lenses, also called telephotos, have a narrower field of view than normal and wide angle lenses, and compress space along the z axis of the frame. Because of this, telephoto lenses appear to bring the background of an image closer to the foreground, flattening space; movement along the z axis is also distorted, so that subjects walking toward of away from the lens look like they are hardly moving. Telephoto lenses flatten facial features, so they are not commonly used for close ups of subjects unless they are only slightly longer than a normal lens. The depth of field

produced by these lenses looks shallow, but there are other factors at play that are examined closer in the depth of field section of this chapter. A good example of a creative use of the telephoto lens can be seen in Stanley Kubrick's *Barry Lyndon* (1975, below); the distortion of distances along the z axis produced by the telephoto is exploited to compress a dense formation of soldiers, emphasizing the cohesiveness, power, and unity of purpose of the advancing Prussian army.

telephoto lens distortion

fast vs. slow lenses

The aperture is the mechanism within a lens which controls the amount of light entering to expose an image on a film frame or CCD sensor. The maximum aperture of a lens (as measured in f-stops), or how much light it lets through when set at its widest opening, forms the basis to classify lenses according to their speed. Lenses with a very wide maximum aperture are called fast, meaning that they require very little light to register an image; for instance, *f* 1.4 or *f* 1.8. Lenses with smaller maximum apertures, like *f* 2.8 and smaller, are called slow, and require more light to register an image. While having a faster lens is invariably a better option, they are much more expensive than slower lenses. On the other hand, they can save you money and time in the long run, since they require less light than slower lenses and let you shoot longer after the sun sets (and way after a slow lens becomes unusable because your light meter tells you to open up to f 1.4).

prime lenses

Lenses that have a single (or fixed) focal length are known as prime lenses. If the quality of the image is the main priority, these lenses are preferred over variable focal length lenses, or zooms, because they can produce better images in terms of contrast, color, and resolution. Primes are also lighter than zooms, because they have fewer internal lens elements. When compared to zoom lenses, primes have a shorter minimum focusing distance, and are generally faster (they have a wider maximum aperture). However, primes are also more time-consuming to use, because they need to be changed every time a different focal length is needed, requiring careful and meticulous handling.

zoom lenses

Zoom lenses are also known as variable focal length lenses, because they have the capability to slide through various focal lengths, often including wide, normal, and telephoto. This is accomplished through a complex mechanism that allows the user to manually adjust the position of elements in the lens housing, effectively changing its optical center. The zoom ratio of a zoom lens refers to its focal length range; a 10:1 zoom means that it can increase its focal length 10 times, going from 12mm to 120mm, for instance. A drawback of using zoom lenses is that because they have more elements than prime lenses, they are slower (the maximum aperture of a zoom lens is always smaller than that of a prime lens). The extra elements in a zoom also tend to produce inferior quality images than those that can be obtained with an

equivalent prime lens. On the other hand, zoom lenses let you work faster because you no longer have to stop shooting every time you need to change the focal length by switching to a different lens. In addition, zoom lenses let you change the focal length even during a shot, which is impossible with a prime lens.

specialized lenses

There are lenses that differ in their construction from primes and zooms, and are generally only used under special circumstances when a specific effect is needed. The tilt-shift lens, for instance, has a movable front element that can be swung, allowing the user to create compositions where two subjects on the same plane of focus will have only one of them in focus. Another specialized lens is the split field diopter, which attaches over your lens and lets you have two subjects at different distances along the z axis in focus simultaneously. A drawback of using this lens attachment is that an area of blurriness is created where the two lenses meet, which filmmakers often conceal by placing it somewhere in the frame where it will not be too evident, as shown in the example from Brian De Palma's *The Untouchables* (1987) below. Other specialized lenses include wide angle and telephoto converters, which attach to the native lens of a video camera to achieve a wider or narrower field of view

split field diopter in action

than the factory lens provides. Although these attachments are relatively inexpensive, there is a clear compromise, since they generally produce images of diminished quality in terms of contrast, color, and sharpness (which becomes even more evident when projected on a large screen). Another kind of specialized lenses include macros, which allow you to focus extremely close to a subject to capture very small details; these lenses are examined further in the macro shot chapter.

depth of field

Depth of field refers to the distance range along the z axis that will be in acceptable focus, meaning sharp. A composition with a deep depth of field has a large area in focus, while a composition with a shallow depth of field has only a small area of the frame in focus. The aperture of a lens is a major factor in manipulating depth of field. Larger apertures that let in more light produce images that have a shallow depth of field, while smaller apertures that let in less light produce images with deeper depths of field. Another way to control depth of field is by changing the distance between the camera and the subject; placing the camera closer to the subject results in a shorter focusing distance, which produces a shallow depth of field. Placing the camera farther away from a subject increases the focusing distance, resulting in a deeper depth of field. If the size of a subject in the frame is kept constant, focal length is not a factor in changing the depth of field. When the size of a subject is not kept constant, increasing the focal length (by using a telephoto lens, for instance) will produce shallow depth of field, while decreasing the focal length (by using a wide angle lens) will produce a deep depth of field. Another determining factor is the size of the shooting format you choose for your project; this is explained in the shooting formats section of this chapter. Being able to produce a shallow depth of field will allow you to isolate your subject in the frame by keeping other visual elements out of focus; this prevents the audience from

shallow depth of field

deep depth of field

being distracted and directs their attention to the subject. Alternatively, a deep depth of field makes every visual element sharp and therefore noticeable by the audience, adding information that can augment their understanding of a subject. Depth of field is one of the most visually expressive and powerful tools you can use to manipulate the composition of a shot. In the two examples above, from Mel Gibson's *Apocalypto* (2006), depth of field is used creatively to indicate the dynamics within a group of Mayan warriors. In the top frame, a shallow depth of field is employed to visually isolate Middle Eye (Gerardo Taracena) after he acted against the will of their leader, Zero Wolf (Raoul Trujillo). In the bottom frame, from later in the film, Middle Eye has stopped questioning his leader and rejoined the group, united behind a single purpose. This dynamic is conveyed visually with the use of a deep depth of field.

camera to subject distance

The camera to subject distance is measured from the film plane, the area inside a camera where the light gathered by the lens reaches the film or the CCD sensor, to the subject, and is used to achieve critical focus (the sharpest possible image). Often, filmmakers will decrease the camera to subject distance to produce a shallower depth of field, although doing this will also change the size of the subject in the frame. Conversely, increasing the camera to subject distance will also increase the depth of field, and decrease the size of the subject in the frame. Using a zoom lens to change the camera to subject distance while maintaining the size of the subject constant will not have an effect in the depth of field, but will affect the perception of it. For instance, a zoom with an aperture setting of f 4 set as a telephoto will appear to have shallow depth of field when compared to the same zoom with the same aperture set as a wide angle. In fact, the depth of field will be practically identical, but since the telephoto lens compresses space along the z axis, the background will appear to be much closer, making it easier to see that it is out of focus.

neutral density filtration

An effective way to control the depth of field in a composition is through the aperture of the lens, but you cannot simply open up or close down without compensating for the light you are losing or gaining as a result, or your exposure will be completely off. When shooting outdoors on a sunny day, it would be impossible to create a shallow depth of field without the use of Neutral Density, or ND, filtration. These filters are calibrated to cut light in precise f-stop increments (cutting light by 1, 2, or 3 f-stops). ND filters work just like sunglasses for your lenses, affecting only the quantity, not quality, of the light that reaches the film or CCD sensor. Using these filters and a depth of field chart (a table that lists the various depths of field that result from a specific camera to subject distance, focal length, and aperture setting), it is possible to accurately determine how many f-stops you need to close down or open up to produce the depth of field you want. When shooting indoors with highly controllable artificial light, it is usually not difficult to shoot with the larger apertures needed to produce a shallow depth field. However, achieving deep depths of field while shooting indoors with artificial lighting poses a problem, because of the extreme lighting requirements necessary to shoot with small apertures. Some professional-grade SD and HD cameras come equipped with internal ND filtration, typically letting you cut light in increments that are equivalent to 3 and 6 f-stops of light (labelled on the camera as 1/8 and 1/64, denoting the amount of light that gets through when the filter is activated).

shooting formats

Your choice of shooting format will have a major impact on many aspects of your visual strategy, but one of the most important has to do with the depth of field you can produce. The smaller the size of the film frame or CCD sensor, the deeper the depth of field will be, and the more difficult it will become to produce shallow depths of field. The reason is directly related to the size of the lens used; smaller formats use smaller lenses, since the area being used to record an image is small. For instance, if you are shooting with 16mm film and you use a 25mm lens (considered a "normal" lens for this format), your depth of field at f 5.6 with a lens focused at 10 feet will be roughly 10 feet. Shooting the same shot with 35mm film, at the same f-stop and camera to subject distance with a 50mm lens (considered "normal" for this format), will yield a depth of field of only 3 1/2 feet. The reason is simple; a 50mm lens for the 35mm film format is physically larger, with a longer focal length than its 16mm equivalent. Now consider SD (standard definition) and HD (high definition) cameras, which use CCD sensors that are many times

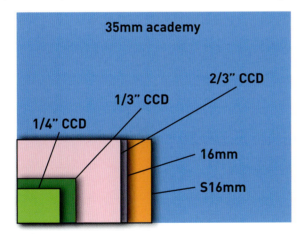

CCD sensors and film format sizes

smaller than a 16mm film frame; the lenses for these video formats are even smaller, and therefore shorter in focal length, than their larger format equivalents (as seen in the illustration above; not actual size, but magnified to illustrate relative sizes). This is the main reason why it is so difficult to create shallow depth of field when shooting with formats smaller than 35mm, especially with video formats that have extremely small CCD sensors. However, we could also reverse this argument, and say that it is very difficult to create deep depths of field when shooting with formats larger than 16mm; you might, for instance, devise a visual strategy that relies on having a deep depth of field, and therefore prefer shooting with a smaller format that will make this possible.

Before the advent of HD video, super 16, or S16, was a popular alternative to approximate the look of 35mm film at a much lower cost. As you can see from the illustration on the left, the frame size is slightly larger than a regular 16mm film frame; this is achieved by using a wider aperture plate that extends to an area of the standard 16mm negative that used to have an optical soundtrack. This results in a frame that uses 20% more negative area, producing an image that has significantly more resolution than standard 16mm. This extra detail becomes crucial when S16 is blown up to 35mm for theatrical distribution (S16 is not a distribution format), since this process tends to magnify grain and any flaws present in the image. S16 is also ideal for HD transfers, because its native 1.66:1 aspect ratio closely approximates the 1.78:1 (or 16x9) aspect ratio of HDTV; regular 16mm has to be severely cropped to fit in this aspect ratio, wasting a large area of the negative and losing resolution in the process. However, the larger size of the S16 format does not bring with it the ability to create shallower depths of field, since its lenses are basically the same size as those used for standard 16mm, producing the same depth of field as a result.

35mm lens adapter kits

A small number of companies have developed lens adapter kits that allow you to attach a 35mm format lens to an SD or HD camera. With these kits, you can produce images with shallow depth of field that would otherwise be very difficult or impossible to produce with video formats. These adapters work by focusing the image from the 35mm lens on a vibrating ground glass; the native lens on your video camera is then focused to record this image. Because 35mm lenses are so much larger than the lens on your video camera (since they were designed to create an image large enough to fill a 35mm film frame), they can easily produce compositions with a shallow depth of field. This, coupled with the higher resolution of an HD camera and 24p progressive shooting, makes it possible to create images that approximate the feel and look of film-originated material (although HD still cannot match the dynamic range or resolution of 35mm film). It is important to take into account that using an adapter will cut a certain amount of light, anywhere from 1/2 to 2/3 of an f-stop. While this might not sound like a lot of light, if you are shooting indoors with artificial light or night exteriors with available light, 1/2 f-stop can be the difference between having a usable image and not being able to shoot unless you have additional lighting. Another important fact to keep in mind is that these adapters usually do not permit you to close down the aperture too much (commonly around f 5.6), or else the texture of the ground glass becomes visible, making your images look like they were shot using a very heavy black pro mist filter with a grainy texture. The shallow depth of field you will get with an adapter will make it more difficult to ascertain critical focus without the use of a large external HD LCD preview monitor; the small LCD flip-out screen that comes with most HD cameras simply does not have the resolution to do this, and can make a slightly blurry shot appear to be in focus. An extremely useful tool to use with a lens adapter kit is a follow focus attachment, which can help you focus quickly and accurately. This geared device attaches a wheel that protrudes perpendicularly to the lens, so that a focus puller (a camera crew member whose job is to maintain focus while taking a shot) can much more easily access and control the focusing ring.

SD and HD video

High Definition, or HD, is rapidly becoming the format of choice for both shooting and broadcasting digital video. Advances in technology are making features that were previously only available on high-end HD cameras (like variable frame rates) available on prosumer (professional-consumer) grade cameras. On the other hand, Standard Definition, or SD, video is slowly but surely being phased out, although

there are still millions of SD cameras out there. Whichever video format you choose for your project, you should be aware of the advantages and shortcomings they will entail. The biggest difference between the SD and HD cameras is, of course, resolution. The standard SD video frame has a resolution of only 720x480 pixels, while HD cameras record frames of 1280x720 and 1920x1080 pixels in size, depending on the camera being used. The higher resolution of HD lets you capture details and render a range of color that is impossible in SD video. This might not be immediately apparent if you are shooting a close up of a subject, but if your composition is a wider shot with a lot of minute details, the extra resolution can make a big difference. Some professional SD and most HD cameras also allow you to capture footage at a 24p, or progressive, frame rate, instead of the standard 30 interlaced frames per second (actually, 29.97 frames per second) which was the only choice for shooting SD video in the past. Shooting at 24p allows the footage to have the same motion artifacts, or degree of blurriness, we have been conditioned to see as "normal" when watching films, since they are also shot at 24 frames per second. Watching side by side identical footage of video shot at 24p and 30i (or interlaced) is startling; even if both videos have the same exact same resolution of 720x480 pixels, the footage shot at 24p will seem

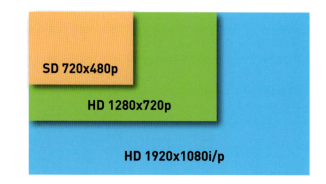

SD and HD frame sizes

much more film-like, since it will not have the added crispness those 6 extra frames per second add.

Prosumer SD and HD cameras also let you control the way the camera responds to light, allowing you to tweak areas of under and overexposure to produce images that have a wider exposure range than what is commonly seen in material shot with less expensive SD cameras. This means that footage shot with cameras that have "gamma compression" or "cine-gamma" settings can produce images that will have a range of tonalities that resemble (although not match) the exposure range of film-originated material. If your aim is to produce footage that will have the feel and look of film without the expense of actually shooting film, then HD video shot at 24p with cine-gamma is your best choice. You might, however, purposely want your footage to have the look and feel of standard SD video, with less resolution than HD, the motion artifacts of 30i, and a narrower exposure range as part of your visual strategy; it worked wonders for Daniel Myrick and Eduardo Sánchez' *The Blair Witch Project* (1999).

Most prosumer and professional video cameras also come equipped with a gain switch, normally with three settings (low, medium, and high), which allows you to boost the sensitivity of the CCD sensor for shooting under low-light conditions. While it might be tempting to engage this switch to shoot under these conditions, you should be aware that using gain invariably adds video noise to your image, even if it is not visible while you are shooting (since the small LCD screens most cameras come equipped with do not have enough resolution to display it). Unless having video noise is part of your visual strategy, you should avoid using gain, and make sure you have sufficient lighting instead.

director's viewfinder

One tool you should try to use as much as possible to train your eye is a director's viewfinder; a small viewing glass that lets you see what the framing of a shot will be depending on the field of view of a given lens and format. Consistently using a director's viewfinder is a good way to become familiar with the aesthetic characteristics of particular focal lengths, specifically field of view, z axis perspective, and apparent motion across the frame. Unfortunately, good director's viewfinders are not cheap, easily costing a few hundred dollars. There are smaller models available, but they have rather small viewfinders that make it hard to see what the frame looks like. If you do invest in one, you will find many opportunities to use it, for instance during preproduction for location scouting (letting you preview potential shots), and during production (letting you quickly select the appropriate lens and position of the camera without having to physically move it). Alternatively, you can also use a digital or even an SLR still camera as a director's viewfinder, provided you know or can calculate the equivalent field of view and focal length of the lens in that camera to the lenses used by the shooting format you choose for your project. Lastly, you can always use your hands to create an ad hoc frame that will let you roughly see what can be included or excluded in a composition. Whichever method you choose, you will eventually become more discriminating about the composition of your shots; your eye will naturally scan the entire frame and not just the focal points, and you will begin to naturally discover visual relationships between elements in your frame that you could not see previously.

a director's viewfinder

1

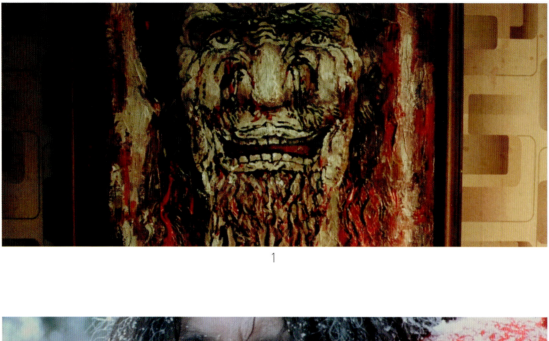

2

Oldboy. *Park Chan-wook, 2003.*

image system

The term "image system" was originally introduced by film theorists, in articles that tried to create a systematic understanding of film through the analysis of images, editing patterns, shot composition, and ideological tendencies of certain directors. In some film theories, image systems are used to decode the layers of meaning a film might have, based on the connotations certain images have in addition to their literal meaning. For instance, a shot of a character looking at his reflection in a mirror can also signify the concept of a divided self and internal conflict, because of the symbolic meanings associated with mirrors and reflections in psychoanalytic theory; this is a common visual trope found in many films dealing with characters who have personality disorders or are suffering internal conflicts. Image system also has a much simpler definition, most often used by filmmakers and screenwriters; it refers to the use of recurrent images and compositions in a film to add layers of meaning to a narrative. The repetition of images can be a powerful tool to introduce themes, motifs, and symbolic imagery that might or might not be explicitly dealt with within the plot of the film. It can also be used to show character growth, foreshadow important information, and create associative meanings between characters that are not explicit in the story. Because the experience of watching a film relies so much on the use of images (although not exclusively, since the film experience always has involved a sound component, even when films were technically silent), most films have an image system at work at some level, whether the filmmaker intends to have one or not. This visual recalling and comparison is inherent in the way audiences extract meaning from images to understand a story, constantly making connections between and within shots. Image systems can be very subtle, repeating certain shot compositions, colors, and imagery in ways that are not easy to notice at first but are nonetheless internalized by the audience on a subliminal level. In this case, only some viewers might notice the repetition of images and shot compositions and infer their narrative significance, decoding an additional layer of meaning to their understanding of the story. Other viewers, however, might completely miss the connections, accessing only the main narrative of a film. Some filmmakers make the image system in their films overt and impossible to ignore, imbuing numerous shots with iconic, graphic, or symbolic significance, sometimes at the expense of letting the audience connect with the story; this is generally not a good idea, since image systems work best when they support and add meaning to, and not become, the point of your film.

Image systems do not have to rely solely on the repetition of images to make a narrative point. An image system could consist, for example, of shots in which the distance between two key characters is gradually diminished (through actual blocking or by using increasingly longer **focal lengths** to visually compress the distance between them along the **z axis**) as their relationship deepens, or shots that gradually switch from high angles to low angles to signal that a character becomes more assertive as the story progresses. An important distinction to keep in mind is that an image system should not be confused with a visual strategy (choices regarding stocks, format, lenses, and lighting). These elements do not constitute an image system, but are instead some of the tools that will make your image system work, in combination with thoughtful shot composition, editing, art direction, and any other element that can be used to develop the explicit and implicit meanings of a shot.

Having an image system is not essential or mandatory; you might not want to deal with having to create one and choose instead to tell your story without any intended extra layers of meaning. On the other hand, coming up with an image system can be a very exciting experience that also helps you get a clearer understanding of your story's structure (necessary to make the image system consistent and meaningful). To create an image system, you must first identify the **core ideas** of your story, its main themes and motifs (something you probably did when you devised the initial concept for the visual strategy of your film). Once you know what your story is really about, you can design an image system that supports your core ideas in overt or subtle ways that should be consistently implemented throughout your film. Consistency is essential if you want the image system to be recognized by the audience; it should be used in a systematic way that underlines only those events that are meaningful to the understanding of the concepts and motifs you want to highlight in your story.

image system in *Oldboy*

Park Chan-wook's *Oldboy* (2006) has an intricate image system that uses the repetition of shot compositions and symbolic imagery to add emotional depth to its story of obsession and revenge. *Oldboy* tells the story of Oh Dae-su (Choi Min-sik), a businessman who gets kidnapped and is then imprisoned for fifteen years; during that time, he learns that his kidnappers have killed his wife and framed him for her murder. Without explanation, Dae-su is suddenly released, befriending a young woman named Mi-do (Kang Hye-jeong) after he passes out at the restaurant where she works. With her help, he finds out his daughter, an infant at the time of his kidnapping, was adopted by a family living in another country. He shortly receives a phone call from the man who imprisoned him, who challenges him to find out the reason behind his kidnapping, giving him a deadline of five days or else he will have Mi-do killed. If he succeeds, the stranger tells him he will kill himself instead. This sets Dae-su on a race against time to save Mi-do and exact revenge on the man who murdered his wife and took fifteen years of his life. With Mi-do by his side, Dae-su succeeds in unraveling the mystery behind his imprisonment; a millionaire by the name of Woo-jin (Yu Ji-tae), who attended the same high school as he, blamed him for the suicide of his sister after Dae-su spread a rumor about their incestuous relationship. Unbeknownst to Dae-su, Woo-jin's revenge had already taken place by the time he finally confronts him, since he had manipulated everything that happened after his release to make him and Mi-do fall in love. In one of the most shocking film endings of the past few years, Dae-su discovers, to his horror, that Mi-do is in fact the daughter he thought had been adopted fifteen years ago, and that Woo-jin's revenge was to have him commit incest with her.

The image system in *Oldboy* is tightly integrated with its narrative; the repetition of compositions and motifs does not work exclusively to add layers of meaning, but is at times an active part of the story, used at key points to advance the plot. For instance, Dae-su discovers that he has had an affair with his daughter through a photo album with pictures of her at different ages that include a photograph he held at the beginning of the film (figure 15), Woo-jin's sister takes a photograph of herself seconds before she commits suicide, which reappears at the end of the film in Woo-jin's penthouse. The repetition motif through the mirroring of events and images are also used throughout the story: Dae-su sees his reflection on the photo album when he uncovers Woo-jin's scheme, Woo-jin's sister stares at her reflection on a mirror while she has an affair with her brother, a hypnotist makes Dae-su use his reflection on a window to erase the memory of his incestuous affair, and Woo-jin's revenge scheme is built around making Dae-su fall in love and commit incest with a family member, mirroring events from his life.

Oldboy also uses repetition in a variety of ways to support the core ideas of the film, amplifying the dramatic impact of the story. Figure 1 shows a painting that Dae-su stares at throughout his imprisonment; it has an inscription that reads "Laugh, and the world laughs with you. Weep, and you weep alone" (a quotation from *Solitude*, a poem by Ella Wheeler Wilcox). After he is released, he recites this line under his breath a number of times, whenever he finds himself in a dire situation usually set up by Woo-jin. The expression on the face in the painting is ambiguous, making it difficult to tell if its subject (a man with wild hair that resembles Dae-su) is smiling or crying. Figure 2 is from one of the last shots in the film, shown after Dae-su has apparently erased the memory of his incest and reunites with his daughter. Like the man in the painting, it is difficult to tell if Dae-su is smiling or crying, suggesting the horrible possibility that he still remembers the incestuous affair he was tricked into having. His grimace would be heart-wrenching to watch even if the audience did not have the context added by its similarity with the face in the painting and the theme of solitude evoked by the poem, but the visual connection between them and the poem makes this moment in the narrative even more emotionally and psychologically complex.

Figures 3 and 4 show Dae-su in the opening scene of the film, in what we later learn is a flashforward, preventing a man from committing suicide. The striking composition of these shots and the questions they generate (who are these men? Why is he trying to kill that man?) make them easy to recall when they are mirrored at the end of the film, through a flashback (keeping with the theme of reflections and mirrored images) that reveals Woo-jin's sister committing suicide under strikingly similar circumstances (figures 5 and 6). The repetition of compositions and circumstances shown here suggests a fateful connection exists between Dae-su and Woo-jin, implying perhaps that in their effort to exact revenge on each other, their obsessive behaviors have made them very much alike. This similarity of behavior is made clear several times throughout the film; Woo-jin goes through an unbelievably convoluted scheme to make Dae-su pay for this transgression, waiting fifteen years until Dae-su's daughter had become a woman to exact his revenge. Dae-su, on the other hand, spends the last ten years of his imprisonment transforming himself into a killing machine, letting go of much of his humanity in the process as he also prepares for revenge. By the time of their final confrontation, their similarity is so pronounced that even the simple act of putting on a shirt is visually connected by the use of almost identical shot compositions and narrative emphasis, with an extreme close up of Dae-su buttoning a cuff (figure 7), that is recreated a few minutes later when Woo-jin is shown doing the same thing (figure 8).

The symbolism associated with certain imagery is also used to establish a connection between characters. Figure 9 shows Dae-su at the beginning of the film, showing off a pair of toy angel wings he bought for his daughter the day of his kidnapping; toward the end of the film, Woo-jin has the wings delivered to Mi-do while Dae-su learns the truth about his relationship with her. She tries the toy wings on and attempts to make them flap, like her father did (figure 10). The repeated action and imagery adds poignancy to the reappearance of the wings (they were finally delivered after fifteen years), while the symbolism associated with angels adds a religious subtext to these scenes; Mi-do and Dae-su have fallen from grace because of the sin they committed and can no longer fly. Religious imagery is also suggested by the reenactment of a painting seen in the prison-room Mi-do stays in while waiting for Dae-su to come back from his confrontation with Woo-jin. A close up of the painting shows a little girl praying (figure 11), a composition that is recreated in a long shot showing Mi-do praying (figure 12). Her connection with the painting in the prison-room also recalls Dae-su's connection with the painting in his own prison-room while he remained in captivity (figures 1 and 2).

Image repetition is also directly acknowledged in the plot, in a scene where Dae-su, following clues left by Woo-jin, visits one of his old high school classmates at a hair salon. While he gets information from her, a young woman enters the shop; Dae-su, who moments before was shown to be strangely attracted to her classmate's exposed knees while she was trying to recall a name, turns his attention to the young woman's knees, shown in a close up (figure 13). Suddenly, the sight of the girl's knees triggers a memory in Dae-su about an encounter he had in high school with Woo-jin's sister, introduced in a flashback also with a close up of her knees (figure 14). Dae-su could not remember this encounter until he saw the girl's knees, suggesting the possibility

that he might have blocked this memory of her because of the psychological trauma he associated with this encounter. This point is reinforced when Dae-su is shown going back to the room where he witnessed Woo-jin and his sister having their incestuous affair. It is only when he revisits the actual spot where he spied on them that he is able to remember the event and finally reveal the reason for Woo-jin's revenge.

The image system in *Oldboy* also uses repetition to show character growth and change. Figure 15 shows Dae-su at the beginning of the film, holding a picture of his family while drunk at a police station; during his final confrontation with Woo-jin, that composition is repeated when he shows him the picture his sister took seconds before her suicide (figure 16). This time, however, Dae-su looks focused, determined, and threatening. He has essentially become a new man, transformed by his ordeal, a change that is also reflected by the blood red shirt he wears here instead of the white shirt he wore at the police station. These two shots also summarize Dae-su's arc in the story: he goes from living an inconsequential and carefree life to living a life filled with purpose (revenge), from taking his family for granted (he gets drunk and arrested on his daughter's birthday) to making them the focus of his life (he plans to avenge his wife's murder and eventually reunite with his daughter), from being an out of shape businessman to becoming a one-man killing machine.

A more typical use of an image system includes the repetition of a particularly easy to remember image toward the end of a film, signaling to the audience that the story has come full circle and is therefore about to end. Figure 17 shows Dae-su being released from his imprisonment early in the film after a hypnosis session, while figure 18 shows him in the last scene in the film, after he wakes from another hypnosis session designed to make him forget the incestuous affair he had with his daughter. The composition of both of these shots is purposely unusual and therefore easy to recall by the audience, with both shots employing a high-angle long shot that shows Dae-su staggering on the ground. This particular use of an image system is very popular among filmmakers, even in films that do not incorporate image systems as intricately as *Oldboy* does. One reason is that repeating images in this way does more than bringing the story full circle; it also gives the audience the impression of narrative closure with no unresolved questions, even if this is not truly the case.

Oldboy has a complex image system expertly interwoven with its narrative, used in a way that amplifies and adds dramatic resonance to the themes and motifs that are already present in its story. This is by far the best way to use an image system, to deepen the emotional impact and audience engagement with a filmic narrative, adding layers of meaning that reward an attentive audience and invite repeated viewings of a film, as new depths, dimensions, and understandings can be gleaned every time the story is revisited. However, the implementation and effectiveness of an image system also relies on the creation of meaningful, narratively compelling compositions for every basic shot of the cinematic vocabulary, the topic of the rest of the chapters in this book.

3

4

5

6

7

8

9

10

Oldboy. *Park Chan-wook, 2003.*

11

12

13

14

15

16

17

18

Sex and Lucia. *Julio Medem, 2001.*

extreme close up

The extreme close up allows you to concentrate the audience's attention on a tiny detail of a character or on small objects. While the **close up** lets the audience see nuances of a performance that would normally be lost in wider shots, the extreme close up can effectively isolate even smaller, single visual details from the rest of the scene. If the detail is extremely small, sometimes these shots are obtained with the use of specialized lenses, and are called **macro shots**, but narratively, they still function as extreme close ups. Using an extreme close up to frame a small object or a detail of a character instantly generates the expectation that what is being shown is important and meaningful to the narrative in some way (an application of **Hitchcock's rule**). Extreme close ups can also be used to make very powerful visual statements within the **image system** of your story. A common use of the extreme close up involves the isolating of an object or a detail of a character that is seemingly unimportant, but ends up playing a critical role later in the narrative. In this case, the extreme close up visually underlines the importance of the object so that its reappearance will not seem unjustified and artificially convenient, and to elicit the audience to anticipate a possible connection as the narrative unfolds. In some cases, the extreme close up works as an **abstract shot**, letting the audience focus on visual details that might not be directly related to the narrative, but nonetheless add to the overall dramatic tone or thematic content because of the abstract or symbolic qualities associated with the image. A good example of this occurs during the opening of David Lynch's *Blue Velvet* (1986), where after a series of shots that include idyllic images of small-town America, the montage ends with an extreme close up of black beetles crawling under a perfectly manicured lawn; the beetles are ultimately irrelevant to the plot, but their appearance within the context of the sequence suggests the thematic idea that primal violence can lurk beneath a surface of idealized social order.

In the example on the opposite page, from Julio Medem's *Sex and Lucia* (2001), an extreme close up is used to concentrate the audience's attention on the path of a single tear as it rolls down the cheek of Elena (Najwa Nimri), a woman who had a torrid affair with a man she met while on a secluded Mediterranean island. The scene opens with a graphic match dissolve from a full moon to a circular pregnancy test with a "plus" sign. Upon seeing it, she sheds a tear that falls on the test, partially smearing the positive result. The visual emphasis the extreme close up places on the tear (because of the closeness of the shot, and by using camera movement to follow its path) imbues this detail with symbolic and even poetic meaning, because of the associations it can elicit (salt water, the sea, tides, moon cycles, menstrual cycles, pregnancy, etc.). In this case, the extreme close up was used to make a thematic point that could only be made with this type of shot.

This arresting extreme close up from Julio Medem's Sex and Lucia *(2001) follows the path of a single tear as it runs down the cheek of Elena (Najwa Nimri), a woman who just found out she is pregnant. The tear, a reminder of the seawater in which her fateful sexual encounter took place, will eventually fall on a pregnancy test.*

why it works

One of the uses of the extreme close up is to make a strong visual statement by concentrating the audience's attention on a small detail of a subject. This usually generates the expectation that this detail will have an important role to play in the larger canvas of the story, even if it is unclear what that will be when the shot is first presented. In this example from Rainer Werner Fassbinder's *The Marriage of Maria Braun* (1979), an extreme close up shows a pack of cigarettes early in the film, after it is established that they are used as cur-

rency in Germany after WWII. At this time in the story it is not clear why this shot (and the narrative emphasis it provides) is being used. At the end of the film, when the title character meets her demise because of a pack of cigarettes, we understand that this extreme close up was actually foreshadowing their importance in the story, adding an element of inevitability to her life, while commenting on the political history of Germany since World War II.

The tight framing of this shot lets you tweak the lighting to make it visually compelling, as long as the overall lighting continuity is maintained. The medium shot that preceded this extreme close up has lighting that comes from a completely different angle, but since the light quality and overall look were maintained, the discrepancy is unnoticeable.

Although this extreme close up contains only a couple of packs of cigarettes, they were arranged within the frame so that they are cropped, suggesting the existence of off-screen space. This is a very common strategy designed to add depth to the composition of a shot.

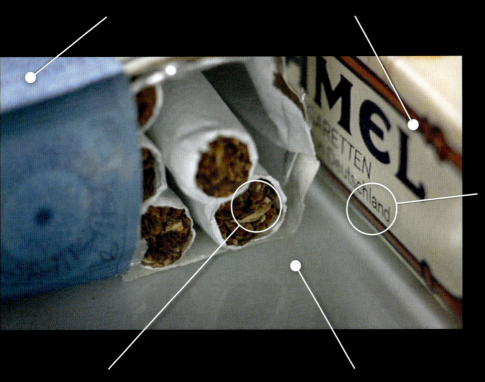

The shallow depth of field allows the selective focusing of important areas of the composition, further adding to the emphasis created by the use of the extreme close up. In this case, the focus was chosen to underline two small details: the word "Deutschland" (Germany) on the pack of cigarettes, and the actual tobacco in the open pack. The symbolism of the American product packaged for German consumption is in line with the political subtext explored in this film.

This cigarette is placed at the focal point of this composition; the diagonals created by the two packs naturally guide the viewer's eye toward it, while the use of shallow depth of field further isolates it from the rest of the frame. The use of these compositional principles to emphasize a seemingly unimportant object inevitably raises certain expectations about the role it plays in the story.

Because an extreme close up can reveal even the minutest details of everything included in the frame, it is a good idea to keep compositions free of any visual elements that might distract the audience from the main subject. The effectiveness of this shot would be severely reduced if, for instance, the cigarettes were resting on a newspaper instead of a white plate.

technical considerations

lenses

Depending on the size of the subject being shot, long **focal length** lenses or **wide angles** are more commonly used. Both lenses can produce **shallower depths of field** (the telephoto because of the optical characteristics inherent to this kind of lens, and the wide angle because of the extremely short distance it will require between the camera and the subject to create a tight framing). **Zoom lenses** are at a disadvantage if they are used as wide angles, since a prime wide angle with the same focal length as a zoom at that setting will be able to focus at a much closer distance, capturing smaller details of the subject in the frame. The native zoom lenses on many **SD** and **HD** cameras also make it relatively easy to shoot extreme close ups, because their shorter focal lengths (the result of the smaller-sized **CCD sensors** they use) allow very short minimum focusing distances. In some cases, the subject might be too small to capture with standard lenses regardless of the format, requiring the use of specialized lenses that allow you to focus even closer than a **prime lens**. Shots that use these lenses are referred to as **macro shots**, because they normally use a macro lens to capture the image (although there are other ways to get the same results; please check out the macro shot chapter for more information).

format

The closeness of this shot sometimes makes it difficult to see all the detail that will be captured, especially when using a wide angle lens that will probably be very close to the subject. In these cases, the use of a large preview monitor can be extremely helpful to see and fully exploit the textures and visual details that an extreme close up will reveal when projected. Shooting film will make using a preview monitor impossible unless you have a film camera equipped with a video assist system that will let you see what the lens is see-ing. **SD** and prosumer **HD** cameras have a slight advantage over film cameras in this regard, since they allow you to preview exactly what the resulting image will look like if you use a preview monitor that approximates or matches the resolution of your **shooting format**. It is best to avoid using the LCD displays that come with most cameras, since they are far too small and lack the resolution and contrast to display every detail being captured. The same cannot be said for film cameras, since even if you were to use an HD-capable monitor to preview the feed sent from a video tap, it would not be capable of displaying the full resolution of negative film stock.

lighting

Whether the subject is a person or an object, lighting should be planned and executed as carefully as if you were shooting a key close up of one of your leading characters. It is easy to forget that although you might be shooting something that is very small, the size of this shot will make a strong visual statement, making it critical that the lighting supports the narrative point being made. The tightness of the framing will most likely preclude the inclusion of light sources that were established in wider shots, giving you license to add, move, and change their direction to produce a shot that is visually compelling, provided that overall lighting continuity is maintained (meaning that you should not suddenly light an extreme close up using a low-key, film noirish look if the wide shot had high-key, soap opera-like lighting, and vice versa). The example from *Clockers* on the opposite page takes full advantage of this freedom to tweak the lighting; although in the preceding wide shots the surrounding area of the interrogation room was clearly visible, in this extreme close up the lighting was adjusted so that only the interrogator's reflection can be seen on the eye, resulting in a visually striking image.

breaking the rules

The tight angles in an extreme close up only allow you to show a tiny detail of your subject, but in this shot from Spike Lee's *Clockers* (1995), the reflective qualities of the human eye are cleverly exploited to include much more. When detective Rocco (Harvey Keitel) interrogates Victor (Isaiah Washington) about the inaccuracies of a murder he has confessed to, he tells him: "I want to see what you see" as this extreme close up is shown. The dramatic lighting in this visually compelling shot was carefully planned so that the detective's reflection would be easy to notice on the pupil of the subject. Interestingly, the word "pupil" comes from "pupilla," the Latin for "little doll," an ancient reference to the very phenomenon captured in this shot.

WALL· E. *Andrew Stanton, 2008.*

close up

The close up is a relative newcomer to the cinematic vocabulary; early silent films used only wide shots and no editing, replicating the experience of watching a staged play. The evolution of the language of cinema and the invention of editing eventually made the close up an essential element of the cinematic vocabulary. The most important feature of a close up is that it lets the audience see nuances of a character's behavior and emotion (especially those that play across the face) that cannot be seen in wider shots. This simple principle has had profound effects on the way films are shot and edited, and in the development of acting for film. Cinematic performance styles quickly departed from the exaggeration expected in the theatre, which was commonplace in early silent films, into a more naturalist style. The closeness and intimacy of a close up lets audiences connect with a character (and a story) on an emotional level in ways that have helped make movies the most popular art form in the world. Filmmakers have found ways to maximize the connection between subject and audience in close ups with the use of visual conventions designed to make the subject the unavoidable focal point of a shot. Technical advancements in lens design, for instance, made it possible to achieve **shallower depths of field**, blurring backgrounds to effectively isolate the subject within the frame, preventing anything from distracting the audience from their emotional investment with characters at that moment in the story. The close up's visual conventions have been so widely adopted that it is relatively difficult to find (although not impossible) a close up with a **deep depth of field**, or a film that does not use them at all. Because of the potential for the close up to elicit the emotional involvement of the audience with a character, its use should be carefully planned for key moments in a story; for example, turning points (instances where a character makes an important decision, usually after discovering or learning something meaningful to them), reaction shots, and P.O.V. shots. If close ups are overused, their dramatic impact will be diluted, making them narratively meaningless within the visual language of your film. Alternatively, close ups are also used when the subject is small enough to require the level of detail this shot size can reveal, or when the importance of an object needs to be conveyed visually (a use of **Hitchcock's rule**).

In Andrew Stanton's *WALL·E* (2008), for instance, we follow the titular character as he goes about his job, collecting and compacting garbage into building-sized piles hundreds of years after humanity has left Earth. As a hobby, he also collects an assortment of items he finds interesting, like spoons, lighters, and toys. One day, he finds a tiny plant (unbeknownst to him an incredibly significant event, since we later learn its discovery means Earth is habitable again). This moment of discovery is punctuated by a textbook example of a close up, carefully composed to underline its importance to the narrative. This close up lets the audience know this is an important event, even if they do not learn why until much later in the story. When used in this manner, the close up can achieve its full narrative potential.

Although completely computer generated, this close up shot from Andrew Stanton's WALL·E (2008) follows virtually every visual convention associated with this kind of shot, from the use of shallow depth of field to subject placement according to the rule of thirds. Can you guess if this is an important moment in the story?

close up

why it works

In terms of connecting with the audience, the close up is one of the most powerful shots used in visual storytelling, and largely responsible for our love affair with movies. When used on a human subject, its main purpose is to let the audience see small nuances of behavior and emotion, so the shot should be composed in a way that excludes or conceals extraneous visual elements that can potentially be a distraction. Depth of field, focal length, lighting, and composition should be carefully manipulated to create an effect of inti-

mate closeness between audience and subject. This close up from the ending of Nuri Bilge Ceylan's *3 Monkeys* (2008), features Eyup (Yavuz Bingol), a man who agrees to take the blame for a fatal car accident after his employer, an influential politician, offers him a large sum of money. The complex psychological state of mind displayed on his face is difficult to define; is he hopeful? Angry? Regretful? Only a close up is capable of conveying such complexity of feeling.

Note how little empty room was placed on this side of the frame when compared to the larger area on the right side. This shot is following the compositional guidelines to maintain proper viewing room for a shot this size.

Why is the head cut off by the top of the frame? Depending on the size of the shot, the amount of headroom must be adjusted accordingly. In this close up, showing the top of the head would result in an uneven, awkward composition. Compare this headroom with the headroom in the medium shot and the medium close up chapters.

In a close up, the eyes of your subject are extremely important; note how the man's eyes have a tiny yet bright reflections shining in them. Without this glint, his eyes would look "dead." Careful positioning of a light or a reflector to add this eyelight is necessary if it does not happen naturally.

The subject is looking toward the right side of the frame; this determines the placement of the looking room area and consequently where the subject should be placed within the frame according to the rule of thirds and the aspect ratio of the format being used. Note how the amount of empty space on the right side of the frame is larger than the one on the left side, properly positioning the subject closer to a sweet spot (although not exactly over it).

The background is usually thrown out of focus by carefully manipulating the depth of field so that it is shallow rather than deep. This is done to prevent anything in the background from distracting the audience from the subject in the foreground.

While the rule of thirds is an excellent guideline for subject placement in many cases, it is not always the "right" way of deciding where to place the focal point of a composition. The headroom is slightly cropped here, placing his eyes a bit high in the frame (according to rule of thirds) that results in a slightly crowded and uneasy composition. The dot marks the exact location of the top left sweet spot for this aspect ratio.

The face of a subject should command the composition of the shot, letting the audience connect to the performance. Anything that can offer a distraction should be avoided; for this reason, most close ups of human subjects are shot using either normal lenses or slight telephotos rather than wide angle lenses that can distort the face.

Another way of manipulating the visual information in the background is to select the appropriate lens to control the field of view, but keep in mind that shorter focal lengths can distort the face of the subject in ways that might be unacceptable to your story.

technical considerations

lenses

Using normal or slight telephoto lenses is the norm, but sometimes wide angles are used when trying to create a distorted view of a character; most often, however, the aim is to avoid anything that will distract the audience from what the subject is feeling, thinking, and seeing. Apertures are normally kept wide to obtain a **shallow depth of field**, blurring the background in the process. When shooting indoors, this is usually not difficult to accomplish since lighting can be easily manipulated (by reducing light output through the use of scrims, and nets, or by repositioning light fixtures) to compensate for the extra light a larger aperture lets in. When shooting outdoors in full daylight, you will need to have a set of **ND filters** handy, which can cut the amount of light entering the lens by several stops, letting you use wider apertures. Note that while you can also manipulate depth of field by changing the distance between the camera and the subject, this might not always be an option when shooting indoors in small spaces; controlling the aperture is often a more effective method.

format

If shooting film, the choice of stock should ideally reflect the creative decisions you made regarding the look of your movie. This means that graininess, color rendition, speed, and contrast should be taken into account when picking a particular stock (in addition to budgetary concerns). Keep in mind that the larger apertures needed to create shallow depths of field when shooting close ups are easier to accomplish with slower, rather than faster, stocks. A faster stock, being more sensitive to light, will force you use a smaller aperture, exactly the opposite you want to do if you need to have a shallow depth of field. If shooting **HD** or **SD video**, it can be especially difficult to achieve shallow depth of field if your **CCD sensors** are on the smaller end (commonly used

in most consumer and prosumer cameras). In this case, you might think about renting or purchasing a **35mm lens adapter kit** for your camera's native lens (and deal with the special requirements its use necessitates). While showcasing detail is one of the aims in a close up, capturing too much detail can sometimes be counterproductive when shooting with some HD formats. Some prosumer HD cameras have a setting that lets you control the amount of detail captured by artificially enhancing sharpness; if this feature is available, you should make sure you are not seeing too much detail in your subject's face, especially when makeup cannot conceal an actor's less-than-perfect skin. This is one of the reasons it is helpful to have a large HD monitor on the set whenever possible, since the small LCD screens in most cameras cannot preview shots with enough detail to assess the result of your settings. It is also important to remember that the close up, regardless of the shooting format, will easily reveal badly applied or excessive makeup, making it necessary to pay special attention to the way it looks in these shots.

lighting

The lighting style you choose for your subject in a close up will depend on the overall visual strategy you have devised; however, it is a common practice to use an eyelight on the eyes to avoid a dead gaze (eyes without a glint in them). This can be easily done by placing a low-wattage light close to the camera so that it glistens in the eyes of the subject (taking care the added light does not undo the look you had set up in wider shots). While overall lighting continuity should be maintained, in a close up you can adjust lights to create a more visually compelling look. Adding a backlight to make the subject stand out in the composition (as seen in the example from *Pulp Fiction*, on the opposite page) is a typical adjustment; this manipulation is less noticeable if the shot you are cutting from (or cutting to) is sufficiently different in angle and size to conceal the change in lighting.

breaking the rules

If the close up's main function is to reveal nuances of behavior and emotion in a subject, what do you make of Marsellus' (Ving Rhames) introduction in Quentin Tarantino's Pulp Fiction (1994)? The director is clearly exploiting and subverting what a close up is supposed to do, by purposely concealing features that would let audiences read this subject's behavioral and emotional cues. Instead, this close up is designed to generate a mysterious and threatening persona around the character of Marsellus, and the inevitable question: what is it with the band-aid on his neck? Note that the rest of the compositional guidelines for a close up are followed (shallow depth of field, rule of thirds subject placement, looking room, headroom), and that the shot never rack-focuses to the famous star sitting in front of Marsellus (which would make this a conventional over the shoulder shot).

Amélie. *Jean-Pierre Jeunet, 2001.*

medium close up

Medium close up shots include a character from the shoulders/chest area up to the top of the head; this shot is tighter than a **medium shot**, but slightly wider than a **close up** (as with all shots that use the human body for reference, the cutoffs between them are not strictly defined). Like the close up, the medium close up showcases the face of a subject, letting audiences see small nuances of behavior and emotion while eliciting a higher degree of identification and empathy; the slightly wider framing also lets body language convey meaning by the inclusion of a character's shoulders. This shot is generally taken with a short **camera to subject distance**, resulting in a **shallow depth of field** that blurs the background to a degree and effectively isolates the character in the composition. Like other shots that include a character and a view of their surrounding area, the medium close up also lets you add dramatic, symbolic, or expository content by what is included in the background; however, since only a relatively small portion of it will be seen, the connection with a character is more direct than in other shots where the background can include more visual elements. This shot's relatively close camera to subject distance means that even a small adjustment in the position of the camera can have a substantial impact on what gets included or excluded from the background. You could, for instance, tilt the camera slightly so that the background of the composition includes a particularly meaningful (to the character or to the audience) prop or color, perhaps as part of the **image system** you created for your story. When used in combination with **long shots**, medium shots, and close ups, medium close ups can convey that something especially meaningful or important is taking place at that moment in a scene. For instance, a conversation between characters could be covered exclusively with long shots or medium shots until someone says or notices something that is significant to a character; at this point a medium close up can showcase a character's reaction, heightening the emotional involvement of the audience with the character and that moment in the scene.

Jean-Pierre Jeunet's *Amélie* (2001), the story of a young Parisian woman (Audrey Tautou) who one day decides to anonymously get involved and help those around her, uses medium close ups throughout the film to underline moments in the story when she decides to help someone or is affected by a discovery she makes about a character, usually unbeknownst to everyone but her and the audience. In the example on the opposite page, Amélie has just learned that the guy she has a crush on is just as quirky and unusual as she is (he collects photographs of footprints on wet cement and works at a carnival's haunted house). The medium close up used here lets the audience notice a quick nervous smile and body language that conveys shyness, revealing how meaningful this information is to her, and setting up the love connection that develops later. Note the inclusion of a blue patch of color at the left of the frame in the background; this is a recurrent visual motif used throughout the film.

The medium close up, like the close up, has the power to increase our emotional involvement, because of the way it centers our attention on every nuance of behavior conveyed by a character's facial expressions; its use throughout Jean-Pierre Jeunet's Amélie *(2001) is one of the reasons audiences were so engaged by its titular character (Audrey Tautou).*

medium close up

why it works

The medium close up showcases the face and shoulders of a character while including a sizable portion of the surrounding area, letting you create compositions that can suggest strong connections between them. This medium close up from Tom Tykwer's *Perfume: The Story of a Murderer* (2006), features Jean-Baptiste Grenouille (Ben Whishaw), a man born with an incredible sense of smell who became a serial killer, moments before his execution. After releasing a whiff of a perfume he created, the mob that was clamoring for his blood only moments before now sees him as an angel sent by God, and is overtaken by his presence. The composition conveys his power over the mob by using a slight high angle that includes a large number of stricken people in the background. He is also placed at the center of the frame, suggesting a strong connection between him and them. The closeness of the shot also lets the audience see the contempt on Jean-Baptiste's face, while the inclusion of his shoulders conveys how relaxed and confident he feels after confirming his newly found power and dominance.

Although not immediately apparent when looking only at the subject, the view behind him indicates this medium close up was shot from a slight high angle, allowing the ground of the plaza behind him to be an integral part of the composition. If a close up had been used instead, this particular subject-background relationship could not have been conveyed in the same way. Interestingly, this composition uses a high angle to make a character look confident and powerful instead of weak, proving that the context of a shot, and not just its composition, create meaning.

The size of the subject in this medium close up requires that the top of his head is cropped to give him the proper amount of headroom. This rule should be followed regardless of the angle at which the shot is taken, unless there is a meaningful reason to ignore it (as shown in the medium shot chapter).

The choice of lens had to account for both the amount of distortion a wider focal length would add to the character's face, and the wide field of view needed to include as many of the seven hundred and fifty extras in the background as possible, emphasizing the magnitude of his power in this scene.

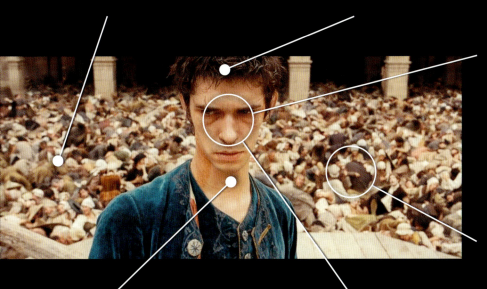

The narrative point made by this shot necessitated a balance between maintaining a shallow depth of field to let the audience focus on the expression on the character's face, while keeping enough visual detail in the background to make it a meaningful part of the composition. Shooting outdoors on a sunny day made it relatively easy for the filmmakers to select an aperture that gave them the depth of field needed to accomplish this effect.

Subject placement did not follow the rule of thirds; instead, he occupies the center of a symmetric composition, creating a static focal point that is suggestive of his power at this moment in the scene. The central placement in the composition also creates a strong visual connection between him and the mob that a few minutes earlier called for his execution.

Although the background is lit by full sunlight, the character does not have any hard shadows across his face, most likely because a butterfly (a large piece of material that diffuses light) was placed directly above him. This is a very common technique used whenever tighter shots of characters are shot outdoors on sunny days.

technical considerations

lenses

Normal and slight **telephoto lenses** are commonly used, since they add little to no optical distortion to the face of a character. Sometimes you might want to purposely add distortion to a composition, using a **wide angle** or an extreme telephoto lens; for instance, if you want to convey that a character is intoxicated, or to exaggerate their movement across the **z** or **x axes** of the frame. Another factor that can determine the use of a particular **focal length** is the amount of the surrounding area you want to include in the composition of the shot, since a medium close up lets you include enough of the background to make it a meaningful element of the frame (as seen in the example from *Perfume* on the previous page). Shorter focal lengths, with their wider fields of view, let you include a wider area along the x axis of the frame and therefore more of the background; conversely, longer focal lengths produce a much narrower field of view, letting you exclude much of it. Note that you will not be able to simply change the focal length without also changing the **camera to subject distance** to maintain the size of a character constant; if you had already framed your medium close up with a normal lens, switching to a telephoto to exclude more of the background will also force you to move the camera farther away from the subject to keep him or her at the same size you had before. While this might not be a problem when you are shooting outdoors and have plenty of room, it might not be so easy while shooting indoors in a tight location with little room to spare. You might also want to choose a focal length to control the apparent distance along the z axis of the frame between a character and the background, using wide angle lenses to extend it (seen in the example from *Perfume* on the previous page) and telephotos to compress it (as shown in the example from *Naked* in the medium shot chapter). Lastly, focal length should not be chosen according to the **depth of field** wanted in the composition; if the size of the subject in the frame and the aperture remain constant, a change in focal length will not affect the depth of field.

format

The main disadvantage of shooting with prosumer **HD** and **SD** video formats is that their smaller **CCD sensors** make it difficult to create shallow depths of field, giving you less control over what the background will look like. Placing the camera closer to the subject while using a long focal length and the largest aperture you can have alleviates this situation somewhat, especially if you are shooting with an HD camera that has a larger sensor and the background is relatively far. Another option is to use a **35mm lens adapter kit** for an HD or SD camera to take advantage of the shallow depth of field of 35mm SLR lenses, but keep in mind that you will have to compensate for the loss of light involved in using a lens adapter.

lighting

When shooting outdoors on a sunny day, it is common to use a butterfly or other kind of diffuser over the heads of actors, to change the quality of the light from hard to soft; this is done to eliminate hard shadows across faces, letting you have more control over exposure and look. There will of course be a difference in the quality of the light between the subject and the background, but this technique is so widely used that most audiences do not notice the discrepancy. Additionally, diffusion material comes in dozens of gradations that can let you control how subtle or severe the change from hard to soft light will be. Shooting indoors with artificial lighting normally involves positioning lights to make your subject stand out in the composition while separating it from the background; this is usually accomplished by using backlights and making sure the subject is slightly brighter than other elements in the frame.

breaking the rules

Medium close ups are generally used in combination with other shot sizes to gradually increase the involvement of the audience when something particularly meaningful takes place in a scene. This medium close up from Tsai Ming-Liang's What Time Is It There? (2001), the story of two young Taiwanese (Lee Kang-sheng and Chen Shiang-chyi, pictured) who share a meaningful connection after a casual encounter, is instead used by itself, without any other shots or action to provide dramatic context. The closeness of the shot lets us connect with the character through the emotions shown on her face, but we are also kept at a distance because we do not know exactly what caused them. This is a common feature of most of Tsai's work, who chooses to emphasize the unity of unfragmented space, time, and performance over narrative clarity.

The Royal Tenenbaums. *Wes Anderson, 2001.*

medium shot

Medium shots typically show one or more characters from the waist up, while still including some of the surrounding area. A medium shot is tighter than a **medium long shot**, but wider than a **medium close up,** although the cutoffs between these shots are not exact. Like the medium long shot, this shot lets you showcase the body language of a character, but the closer perspective also lets the audience see some facial nuances of behavior and emotion. When they include more than one individual, medium shots can convey the dynamics of a relationship through character placement in the composition in addition to their body language. This is one reason why they are often used for **two shots**, **group shots**, and **over the shoulder shots**. Since medium shots are wide enough to include some of the location in the frame, it is important to be aware that the arrangement of subjects in the composition can be used to suggest a connection to that space. Also, because the medium shot can contain a lot of visual detail, it normally needs to stay longer on the screen than tighter shots that have less information. Medium shots are useful as transition shots between wider, more expository shots, and tighter, more intimate shots, allowing you to gradually increase audience involvement. A common scenario involves using medium shots to cover a conversation between two or more characters until a key moment occurs; at this point, a medium close up or a close up is used, adding dramatic emphasis to the moment. Then, after this beat, the rest of the conversation returns to medium or wider shots. The added emphasis provided by the tighter framing of the close up or medium close up only works because wider, expository shots, like the medium shot, are used to establish facts of the scene, locale, character, and physical relationships, before a change in the dramatic direction of the scene

is introduced. Of course you could also cut directly from long shots to close ups, bypassing the use of medium shots altogether; in this case the drastic change in angles would be read by the audience as a drastic change in dramatic direction, which might be exactly what you want depending on the needs of your story.

Wes Anderson's films are known for their elaborate and imaginative art direction, costume design, and oddball characters; unsurprisingly, medium shots that showcase them prominently are used extensively in most of his films. In this typical medium shot from *The Royal Tenenbaums* (2001, on the opposite page), Margot Tenenbaum (Gwyneth Paltrow), an adopted member of the titular family, hides from her husband to smoke a cigarette. The relatively wide area covered by the shot, coupled with carefully chosen lighting, depth of field, wardrobe, body language, and central placement of the character in the composition, allows the audience to make connections between her and the various items around her (the darkroom paraphernalia, the animal motifs on the wallpaper, the pink telephone) that convey a lot of specific information about her character in a single image.

The predominant use of medium shots in Wes Anderson's The Royal Tenenbaums *(2001) showcases characters and locations almost equally, conveying a lot of information about their personality quirks, hobbies, and careers to the audience.*

medium shot

why it works

The relatively wide field of view of a medium shot is ideal for establishing visual relationships between characters, and between characters and their surroundings. In this example from Mike Leigh's *Naked* (1993), we see Johnny (David Thewlis), a well-read but misanthropic homeless man who lives his life on a self-destructive path, extracting joy out of ranting at strangers, as he aimlessly wanders the streets of London. The simple composition of this medium shot perfectly encapsulates how Johnny sees himself and the reality of his situation, placing him slightly above the people who go about their business with purpose, while he, with nowhere to go, watches them snidely. This shot is also an example of an emblematic shot, since it conveys many of the core ideas explored in this film within a single image.

The pedestrians were placed a few inches lower than the character at the focal point of the composition, making it easier for the audience to notice his facial expressions even when they cross the foreground. Although the medium shot showcases body language and location, it is still possible to convey emotions through the face of a character, especially if the composition makes them easy to see, as in this case.

The placement of this character follows the rule of thirds, giving him the proper amount of headroom for a frame with this aspect ratio. The arrangement of visual elements in this composition was also designed to isolate him in this area of the frame, by making sure nothing else around him can distract the audience from noticing his reactions to the passing crowd below him.

The pedestrian traffic crossing the frame from both sides adds multiple layers of depth to the composition, while creating a sense that space extends beyond the edges of the frame. Their movement also provides a sharp visual contrast against the stillness of the character at the focal point of the composition, making him stand out even more, leading the audience to focus their attention on him.

The shallow depth of field in the foreground of the image lets the audience concentrate their attention on the main subject of the composition; the use of a telephoto lens coupled with a larger aperture helped achieve this effect. Using a telephoto lens also allowed the camera to be placed relatively far from the subject, making it possible to get this shot without alerting the passerby.

The compression along the z axis of the frame seen here suggests the use of a telephoto rather than a normal or wide angle lens. Since this shot was taken outdoors, it was possible to place the camera far from the subject to get this relatively narrow field of view. Getting the same composition while shooting indoors with the same lens would probably not have been possible because of the space needed, forcing the use of a wider lens instead.

technical considerations

lenses

The size of this shot normally showcases both a character and the immediate area, so your lens choice should take into account the kind of spatial relationship you want to establish between them. For instance, you might want to create a medium shot that makes the location visible behind the subject look as if it is far away in the background; in this case, you could use a **wide angle lens**, since it can make distances along the **z axis** appear to be longer than they really are. Conversely, you could achieve the opposite effect, and make it look as if the background is very close to the subject, by using a **telephoto lens** to compress the distance along the z axis. Of course, you can also control what gets noticed besides the character (or instead of it) by manipulating the **depth of field**, making sure only certain visual elements are within the range of sharp focus; to do this, you must have control over the lighting so that you can open up or close down the aperture of your lens, whether you are shooting indoors or outdoors. While the **field of view** of this shot can be obtained with almost any lens, be it a wide angle, **normal**, or telephoto, the size of the location will sometimes force you to use one lens over another. For instance, if the medium shot is taken indoors, in an apartment or a bathroom, and you want to use a telephoto lens for aesthetic reasons, you might not have enough room to place the camera far enough to include the subject from the waist up as a medium shot requires; instead, you will be forced to use a normal or most likely a wide angle lens, because of the wider field of view it can capture at close distances.

format

If you want to manipulate depth of field to control what details will be seen in a medium shot, be aware that the smaller **CCD sensors** of most consumer and prosumer **SD** and **HD** cameras will make it nearly impossible to achieve shallow depth of field, because of the smaller, comparatively wider angle lenses they use. Since there is a minimum **camera to subject distance** you need to have to achieve a medium shot, you will not be able to get close enough to the subject to manipulate depth of field this way, and in most cases you will end up having sharp focus from the foreground to deep in the background. The use of a **35mm lens adapter kit**, available for some HD and SD prosumer cameras, will give you control over the depth of field, but you will have to be prepared to compensate for the light it cuts, especially when shooting indoors.

lighting

Since medium shots allow you to include a portion of a location in addition to a character in the frame, lighting can be used to reveal, conceal, or showcase either one, depending on the needs of your story. A common strategy when lighting medium shots (and generally any shots that include characters and locations) is to make the subject stand out by separating it from the background with the use of a backlight, and by ensuring that it is one of the brighter visual elements in the frame. Background and foreground visual elements are normally kept darker than the subject; how much darker will depend on how much you decide should be visible to the audience, and can vary from less than one f-stop (the smallest difference in brightness the human eye can perceive) all the way to complete underexposure. Check out the difference in brightness between characters and backgrounds in the medium shots from *The Royal Tenenbaums* on the first page, and *Jeanne Dielman, 23 Quai du Commerce, 1080 Bruxelles* on the opposite page; the slightly brighter Margo Tenenbaum was lit to stand out from the background, while Jeanne Dielman appears to blend with it, suggesting two very different kinds of relationship between subject and surrounding area.

breaking the rules

Chantal Akerman's minimalist masterpiece *Jeanne Dielman, 23 Quai du Commerce, 1080 Bruxelles* (1975), examines three days in the life of Jeanne (Delphine Seyrig), a young widow, as she performs daily house chores that include the turning of tricks to make ends meet. The film uses static long takes and repetitive medium and long shots, with compositions that seem to document, rather than dramatize, Jeanne's domestic routines. In this medium shot, the composition crops her head from the frame as she greets a client, an unusual formal transgression; this simple compositional choice has profound narrative implications in the relationships it suggests between the titular character and the home she maintains throughout the film.

Leon: The Professional. *Luc Besson, 1994.*

medium long shot

Medium long shots include a character or characters from approximately the knees up in the frame; they are wider than **medium shots**, but tighter than **long shots**. These shots are also sometimes known as "American shots," originally named by European critics because they were first introduced in early American western films (according to film history lore, this shot size was created to include characters and their gun holsters). Medium long shots are commonly used for **group shots**, **two shots**, and **emblematic shots**, because they provide enough room in the frame to include several characters or visual elements simultaneously. While the long shot emphasizes the body language of a character and the surrounding area, the size of the medium long shot allows you to showcase body language, some facial expression, and the surrounding area simultaneously, making them ideal for situations when a relationship between these three visual elements needs to be established to present a narrative or expository point to the audience. The size of a medium long shot is also ideal to establish the dynamics of a relationship between characters, by the way they are placed within the composition (by using **Hitchcock's rule**, or **balanced/unbalanced** framings, for instance). Like long shots and medium shots, medium long shots are commonly used in combination with tighter shots to control the emotional involvement of the audience (normally by cutting to medium close ups or close ups at key moments of a scene), but because they can pick up some facial expression, medium long shots can also be used by themselves without completely sacrificing the kind of emotional connection that is associated with tighter shots. The relatively wide coverage of medium long shots makes it necessary to keep them on the screen slightly longer than tighter shots with fewer visual elements,

especially when they are used at the beginning of a scene to set up the spatial relationships between characters or between characters and their surrounding area.

The medium long shot on the opposite page, from Luc Besson's *Leon: The Professional* (1994), features a small exchange between the titular character (Jean Reno), an expert hitman, and Mathilda (Natalie Portman), a 12 year old he saved from a gang of corrupt cops. In the previous scene, Mathilda proved her intent to become a killer by blindly shooting a gun out of his apartment's window, prompting Leon to move out. The medium long shot that follows is used as a reveal: Leon appears first in the frame as he walks toward us, tricking the audience into thinking he has ditched Mathilda. As the shot continues, Mathilda enters the frame revealing that he has in fact decided to let her tag along. The scene plays out entirely in this shot as they have a brief exchange, relying on the ability of the medium long shot to show some facial expression and much body language. The central placement of the characters in the frame, combined with the exclusion of most of the background and the use of **shallow depth of field**, isolates them from their surroundings, underlining the awkwardness of their pairing by letting the audience concentrate on their dramatically contrasting costumes and physical appearance.

A medium long shot perfectly showcases the differences in height, physical appearance, and wardrobe between Mathilda (Natalie Portman) and Leon (Jean Reno) in this exchange from Luc Besson's Leon: The Professional *(1993).*

medium long shot

why it works

The size of a medium long shot is ideal to showcase a character's body language, some facial expression, and the surrounding area simultaneously, a characteristic used to maximum effect in this example from the poignant ending of Michael Radford's adaptation of George Orwell's dystopian *Nineteen Eighty-Four* (1984). The composition of this shot is designed to let the audience see Winston Smith (John Hurt), a Party worker at the Ministry of Truth, after he was tortured and brainwashed for committing a thoughtcrime (keeping a diary). He is flanked by a poster with the figurehead of the state, Big Brother, and a telescreen that plays his confession as traitor to the Party. A long shot would not have allowed us to see the listless expression on his face, while a medium shot would have excluded either the poster or the confession, both necessary visual elements to communicate the narrative point of this shot. Note the use of extra headroom over the character, visually emphasizing his defeat by the totalitarian regime that watches over his every move, symbolized by the gaze of Big Brother behind him.

This poster, showing the penetrating gaze of Big Brother, was carefully placed within the composition so that it would appear to look down on the next move by the character at the center of the frame, symbolizing the constant surveillance of the state over the activities of its citizens.

This is an excessive amount of headroom for a shot this size, but within the context of this scene it conveys the character's defeat and submissiveness under the gaze of a poster showing Big Brother behind him.

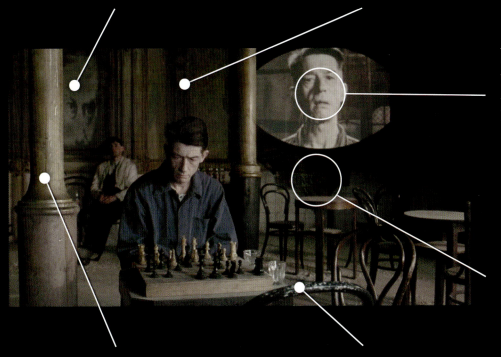

The inclusion of this telescreen in the background is essential to the narrative point being made by this shot. Seeing this character confess to crimes he did not commit while he sits reactionless in the foreground confirms that the confessions shown throughout the film were also untrue, staged by the state after torturing and brainwashing its citizens.

The camera to subject distance, focal length, and depth of field were carefully chosen to make sure all the visual elements necessary to make this shot work are included in the composition, and sharp enough to be clearly identified by the audience.

The inclusion of this column in the foreground adds depth to the frame by implying the existence of off-screen space; it also provides a depth cue of relative size when compared to the column in the background.

Although this chair is only partially protruding into the frame, it functions as a repoussoir, an object that adds depth and leads the viewer's gaze toward the center of the composition.

technical considerations

lenses

Because the medium long shot can include a character's body language and some facial expression along with the surrounding area, the choice of lens can be especially critical, since it can be used to include or exclude visual elements from the frame according to the **field of view** needed. The example from *Leon: The Professional* at the beginning of this chapter, for instance, deftly uses a **telephoto lens** to exclude a lot of the background, directing the audience to concentrate solely on the two characters and their exchange at that time. A very different kind of relationship between character and surrounding area is established in the example from *Nineteen Eighty-Four* on the previous page, where a lens with a **focal length** much closer to normal was used, allowing a large portion of the location to be included in the composition (although not as much as would be included if a **wide angle lens** had been used). In this shot, allowing the audience to see the area surrounding the central character is essential to establish the multiple visual and thematic relationships contained in this complex moment. Focal length can also be selected according to the need for either **shallow or deep depth of field** in the composition. Actual control over the range of focus will of course be more a function of the aperture and not the focal length, but depending on the distance between foreground and background visual elements, a shallow depth of field will be easier to achieve with a telephoto lens (since it compresses distances along the **z axis**) than a wide lens (since it expands distances along the z axis).

format

Any type of shot that depends on the manipulation of depth of field to establish a visual relationship between characters or between a character and the surrounding area will benefit from the flexibility of being able to use interchangeable lenses, possible only when shooting film or **HD** and **SD** video with the use of a **35mm lens adapter kit**. **SD** cameras and their native zoom lenses make it very difficult to create any composition with a shallow depth of field. Shots that require deep depth of field, however, will not present a problem when shooting with an SD video camera, since the smaller native lenses they use produce inherently deeper depths of field.

lighting

The relatively wide field of view in a medium long shot might necessitate the use of larger lighting instruments when shooting indoors, especially if the composition precludes the placement of lights close to the subject. For instance, in the example from *Nineteen Eighty-Four* on the previous page, a single light source had to be powerful enough to reach all the way to the back wall. The size of this shot might also prevent you from placing butterflies over the subjects when shooting on sunny day exteriors to control the quality of the light, a very common technique used in medium shots and medium close ups (as seen in the example from *Perfume: The Story of a Murderer*, in the medium close up chapter). Shooting night exteriors will require powerful lights that will most likely necessitate using a portable generator, or finding a location that has available light that is bright enough to achieve a usable exposure. This problem is exacerbated when shooting **SD** or **HD** video since their **CCD sensors** are less sensitive to light than fast film stocks.

breaking the rules

Medium long shots are generally used to showcase a character and some of the surrounding area, but in this example from Bong Joon-ho's Memories of Murder (2003), a film based on the true story of South Korea's first serial murders, a character who fears she is being stalked by a killer is purposely kept out of focus throughout the length of the shot, diverting the audience's attention to the deserted woods around her instead. This unusual and highly effective technique shifts the focus both figuratively and literally away from the human subject to the deceptively harmless woods before the character is violently attacked by the serial killer. Note that although the character is completely blurred, she was placed in the composition according to the rule of thirds, ensuring a dynamic frame and the proper amount of headroom for a medium long shot.

Sid and Nancy. *Alex Cox, 1986.*

long shot

The long shot includes characters in their entirety in the frame, along with a large portion of the surrounding area. While there can be a main subject in a long shot, the perspective is too remote to see emotional detail on the face. This shot concentrates on the body and what it reveals. Like **extreme long shots**, long shots are commonly used as **establishing shots**, placed at the beginning of scenes to let the audience know where the action that follows will take place. Sometimes, long shots are also placed at the end of a scene, usually with a composition that conveys a different dramatic tone from the one established at the beginning of the scene, marking a change in the emotion or outlook of a character. Like **medium shots**, the composition of long shots can be made to: emphasize a character while neglecting the space around them, emphasize the space over the character, or to establish a special connection between a character and the space around them. The wide **field of view** of long shots also makes them ideal for the **emblematic shots** (shots that convey complex, associative ideas by the arrangement of visual elements in the frame). The size of this shot also works well for **group shots**, providing enough room in the frame to imply power dynamics between characters. Because the long shot can contain many details and visual elements, it is normally kept longer on the screen than other shots that have less information. This extra duration gives the audience enough time to register everything there is to see. Used in conjunction with medium shots, **medium close ups**, and **close ups**, long shots are also commonly used to gradually increase the emotional involvement of the audience, by, for instance, covering a scene with long shots and medium shots until something important takes place, at which point medium close ups and close ups are used. Alternatively, since long shots are not ideal to showcase the facial expressions of a character, they can also be used to limit the emotional involvement of the audience, preventing them from seeing emotional cues they would normally get with a close up or a medium close up.

Alex Cox's biopic *Sid and Nancy* (1986), a film that follows the mutually destructive relationship that existed between Sex Pistols' bassist Sid Vicious (Gary Oldman) and an American groupie, Nancy Spungen (Chloe Webb), features long shots that consistently place them amidst the drugs, alcohol, violence, and filth that permeated their world. In the example on the opposite page, a mesmerizing long shot (also a perfect example of an emblematic shot) that perfectly captures the alternate nature of their punk rock lifestyle and romance, they are shown semi-silhouetted in a filthy alley, kissing lovingly as garbage rains down in slow motion. The composition places them against a gap between buildings which makes them stand out in the frame, emphasizing the contradiction between their actions (a loving kiss) and the setting. Not surprisingly, this arresting image was also used in one of the promotional posters for the film.

This visually stunning long shot from Alex Cox's Sid and Nancy (1986) makes a powerful statement about the unorthodox relationship that existed between punk rocker Sid Vicious (Gary Oldman) and his girlfriend Nancy Spungen (Chloe Webb).

why it works

In addition to conveying relationships between characters and their surrounding area, the long shot can be used to suggest narrative and thematic dynamics between characters, through their placement and relative scale in the composition. The wide area covered by this shot makes compositional guidelines like Hitchcock's rule, balanced and unbalanced frames, and the compression/expansion of space along the z axis, particularly helpful in establishing these relationships.

In this long shot from Lana and Andy Wachowski's *The Matrix Reloaded* (2003), an impending fight between Neo, (Keanu Reeves) a man prophesied to liberate humanity from the rule of intelligent machines, and Agent Smith (Hugo Weaving), a program that polices the virtual reality called "The Matrix," is suggested by their placement in the composition as a duel of equally matched opponents, increasing the tension and dramatic impact of the scene.

Lighting was manipulated so that both characters have a backlight that separates from the background to make them stand out in the composition. This is a very common practice designed to guide the viewer's gaze toward the most important area in the frame, usually a character.

The amount of headroom in this composition is correct for a shot this size; increasingly tighter framings should have increasingly smaller amounts of headroom (as seen in the medium close up and close up chapters). Alternatively, headroom can also be purposely exaggerated or removed altogether to make a narrative point about a character.

Characters were not placed in the frame according to the rule of thirds; instead, they were placed unusually close to the edges of the frame, emphasizing the empty space between them while almost completely removing the space behind them. This placement in the composition implies they can only move toward each other, foreshadowing their imminent fight.

The framing of this shot shows both characters taking up the same amount of room in the frame, suggesting that they are evenly matched; this is a typical implementation of Hitchcock's rule. Their placement in the frame also creates a balanced composition, further emphasizing their equal power, increasing the tension and suspense of the scene.

The composition of this shot has only two layers of depth: the foreground where the characters are placed, and the background. The lack of a third layer creates a somewhat flat composition, visually restricting character movement to the x axis of the frame, toward each other and conflict. The use of a closed framing also reinforces their lack of options by excluding off-screen space.

The background is a couple of f-stops darker than the characters in the foreground, making them the focal points of the composition and ensuring that the audience's attention will be on them. This is a very common lighting strategy whether the shot is indoors or outdoors, day or night.

technical considerations

lenses

Like all wide **field of view** shots, the long shot can establish a relationship between a character and the surrounding area, adding emotional or dramatic content that might be explicitly addressed in the narrative or implicitly suggested solely through the composition of the shot. Because of this, the choice of **focal length** can have a dramatic impact in the way the audience makes visual connections between character and location. A **wide angle lens**, for instance, can distort perspective to make the surrounding area appear be to larger and more distant than it is, visually disconnecting a character from it. Conversely, a **telephoto lens** can bring the background behind a character uncomfortably close, establishing a strong visual connection between them. Keep in mind that if the long shot is taken indoors, you might not have enough room to use a telephoto lens, because of the extreme **camera to subject distance** you need to include the entire character in the frame. Whichever lens you choose, remember that the connections the audience will make between character and location will also be greatly influenced by where you place the character in the composition of the frame; this placement and the focal length you choose should complement, and not work against, each other.

format

The longer camera to subject distances needed to include a character in his entirety in the frame exacerbate the problems inherent in achieving a shallow depth of field with the smaller lenses of most consumer and prosumer **SD** and **HD** cameras. It will be virtually impossible to get a soft background while shooting with these formats at these distances, even with a wide open aperture. One option is to get a **35mm lens adapter kit**, which can let you use regular 35mm SLR lenses in front of the native lens of your camera. Unfortunately, compensating for the light the adapter will cut can

be more difficult with this type of shot, since you will have to light a much larger area than in tighter shots. Film formats have the inherent advantage of making it easier to achieve shallower depths of field because of their larger lenses, although for the same reasons it is more difficult to achieve deeper depths of field in 35mm than in the **16mm** film format.

lighting

Another way to control the visual relationships between characters and location in a long shot is to restrict the amount of detail that can be seen in the background by controlling the **depth of field**; this is best accomplished through the aperture of your lens, which can be manipulated if you have control over the lighting and the sensitivity of your shooting format. One strategy is to reduce the distance between camera and subject as much as possible while still including the subject's entire body (otherwise it would not be considered a long shot) coupled with a large aperture and a telephoto lens. If shooting outdoors in sunlight, you will have to use **ND filtration** to block enough light to use a large aperture. If you are shooting indoors with artificial light and want a deep depth of field, be prepared to have a lot of lights so that you can use the smaller apertures to achieve it. Note the shallow depth of field in the example from *Sid and Nancy*, where the subjects are closer to the camera while still in a long shot, versus the deep depth of field in the example from Michael Haneke's *Hidden* (2005) on the opposite page, where the subjects are farther away from the camera. Lighting is also especially important to make the subject stand out in the composition so that the audience's gaze is directed toward it. The convention is to light subjects so that they are brighter than the surrounding area, although sometimes the same effect can be achieved by silhouetting them instead, making sure the surrounding area is brighter, as seen in the *Sid and Nancy* example.

breaking the rules

The distance necessary to include characters in their entirety makes the long shot less than ideal to showcase nuances of behavior and emotion through facial expressions, which sometimes can be exploited to add suspense and tension to a scene. Michael Haneke's appropriately titled Hidden (2005), follows the story of Georges (Daniel Auteuil), a TV personality who suddenly gets stalked and harassed by someone he assumes is tied to a transgression he committed as a child. In this long shot, the final image from the film, we see his son Pierrot (Lester Makedonsky) chatting with the son of the man who might have been behind the harassment (Walid Afkir). The cluttered mise en scène makes it hard to notice them at first, and later difficult to see the exact nature of their relationship, preventing the audience from unraveling the mystery and getting narrative closure, a recurrent technique used throughout this film.

Last Year at Marienbad. *Alain Resnais, 1961.*

extreme long shot

The extreme long shot lets you create compositions that emphasize the scale of a location. When human subjects are included in the frame, they usually occupy a very small area, and are dwarfed by their surroundings. Sometimes extreme long shots do not have a character in the frame; in this case they showcase the location itself, and are referred to as **establishing shots**. It is common to use establishing shots at the beginning of a scene, to let the audience know where the action that follows will take place. Another common practice is to use extreme long shots to suddenly reveal the vastness or character of a location, usually after the use of a **close up** where a subject reacts to something they can see but the audience cannot, heightening tension and suspense (a favorite Spielbergian device). Extreme long shots are also ideal to showcase spatial relationships and interactions between large groups of people, for instance during large battle scenes. While the perspective of shots from medium to **extreme close up** restrict the amount of visual information to a single subject, or even just an aspect of a single subject, the extreme long shot lets you establish visual relationships between several characters and characters and their environment. Compositional guidelines like the **rule of thirds**, **balanced/unbalanced** compositions, and **Hitchcock's rule** are especially useful in the arrangement of visual elements in the frame. The wide **field of view** of these shots also provides enough room to contain several visual elements in the frame, making them ideal to create **emblematic shots**. The **depth of field** in these shots is usually deep, a function of the long **camera to subject distances** necessary to include a location and its surroundings. It is also important to remember that the amount of visual information a shot of this size can contain will normally take more time for the audience to fully register, making it necessary to keep the shot on the screen longer than other shots that contain less information. When characters are included in the frame, the composition of the extreme long shot is usually designed to let the audience compare the difference in scale between them and a location, so it is important that they are arranged within the composition in a way that will make them easily noticed.

Alain Resnais' enigmatic *Last Year at Marienbad* (1961), has a famous extreme long shot that deftly exploits the guidelines of composition to create a memorable image, as seen on the opposite page. This shot, one of many fascinating and baffling visual puzzles in the film, has a symmetric composition that underlines the geometric patterns of an opulent garden, disturbed only by a number of characters standing motionless (like the statues around them) on a path at its center. Strangely, they cast long shadows on an overcast day (at an angle that breaks the order established by the rest of the visual elements in the frame), adding a surrealistic touch to the oneiric tone of the film. Only an extreme long shot could have simultaneously included all visual elements (garden, people, and sky) necessary to convey the narrative point of this shot.

This extreme long shot from Alain Resnais' Last Year at Marienbad (1961) has puzzled audiences for decades. The symmetrical framing of the garden, possibly hinting at the inexorability of destiny, is disturbed by visitors who are strangely capable of casting shadows on an overcast day.

extreme long shot

why it works

The extreme long shot is ideal to display a vast field of view that emphasizes the scale of a location. If a subject is included in the frame, it occupies a very small area and is usually placed in a way that will let the audience easily notice the contrast in sizes. Extreme long shots can also be used as establishing shots, inserted at the beginning of a scene to introduce the audience to a location where the rest of the action will take place. This extreme long shot from Francis Lawrence's *I am Legend* (2007) shows Robert Neville (Will Smith) going about a normal day as the last survivor of a plague that killed every human in New York City in 2009. The wide field of view of this shot dramatically reveals an impossibly deserted Fifth Avenue in Manhattan (made empty with the aid of CGI), and is one of several extreme long shots designed to convey the broad and total devastation caused by the plague and the loneliness and isolation felt by Dr. Neville as the last human survivor left in the city.

The wide angle lens used to shoot this composition added some distortion to the image, evidenced by the warping sides of the buildings that are closer to the edges of the frame and the convergence of architectural lines towards the horizon. It also exaggerated the distances along the z axis, in this case to showcase the complete absence of traffic and people along the avenue.

The horizon line was framed so that it rests on the bottom third of the frame, its more conventional location according to the rule of thirds. This area of the frame is also the main focal point; note how the architectural lines of the buildings naturally lead the eye toward it, further emphasizing the vast stretch of emptiness along the normally crowded avenue.

Note that while the character was placed off-center, he is moving towards one of the sweet spots created by the division of the frame into thirds; the entrance to the museum, his destination in this shot, is directly over the lower left sweet spot.

The character is easily noticeable even in this extreme long shot because of the especially bright steps, a result of the angle at which sunlight is illuminating them. If the character were going up the darker side stairs or was walking across the shadowed street, we would not notice him as easily.

The inclusion of this lamp post in the foreground provides both a visual cue of relative size that accentuates the z axis (when compared to the receding lamp posts in the background), and implies the existence of off-screen space beyond the borders of the frame.

Although he occupies a very small area in the frame, the dark clothing worn by the character makes him stand out against the light-colored steps of the Metropolitan Museum of Art; he is also the only element in this composition that moves across the frame, making it very easy for audiences to notice him even in this detail-heavy composition.

technical considerations

lenses

Extreme long shots benefit from the use of **wide angle lenses**, which provide wider **fields of view** and exaggerate the depth of the frame along the **z axis**, emphasizing the scale of subjects placed along it. It is also possible to use **telephoto lenses** for certain compositions when compression along the z axis is desired, but these lenses restrict the field of view and are therefore less capable to showcase the broader x axis vistas usually associated with extreme long shots. Apertures will normally be small, since most of the time these shots will be taken outdoors in daylight. Night exteriors, unless shot with available light, or as day for night or dusk for night, will be very expensive to light. While **ND filtration** can allow you to use wider apertures, these shots normally involve very long **camera to subject distances**, which result in deep **depths of field** (there are, however, special **tilt-shift lenses** that allow you to selectively shift the focus to either side of the frame over a single plane, creating the illusion of shallow depth of field if needed). The smaller format lenses found in most consumer and prosumer **SD** and **HD** cameras have an inherent advantage in this respect, making it relatively simple to compose very wide shots because of the shorter focal lengths of their native lenses.

format

Depending on the amount of visual information included in the frame, formats capable of higher resolutions (like film and higher end HD cameras) will do a better job with extreme long shots that have many small details, like an extreme long shot of a crowded city street with lots of vehicles and pedestrians. Lower resolution formats (like SD video and lower-tier HD) will be unable to render minute detail because of their inherent lower resolution, and because of the compression algorithms their formats use to record the footage. Sometimes filmmakers mix formats because of the

resolution requirements of a particular shot; Fernando Meirelles and Kátia Lund, for instance, used both the **Super 16** (for close ups of actors) and the Super 35 mm (for extreme long shots of the favelas) film formats in their acclaimed film *City of God* (2002).

lighting

Unless you have access to very powerful lights and the cranes needed to hoist them high in the air, you will most likely not be shooting extreme long shots outdoors at night. In rare circumstances, you might be able to use available light that happens to be strong enough to expose an image using film stock or digital video; for instance, by shooting under the bright lights used in some outdoor parking lots. There are options for shooting what appear to be night exterior shots, however, by shooting day for night or dusk for night, but they can severely restrict your framing by preventing you from including the sky in the shot (which would look too bright for a night shot and immediately give away the trick). Otherwise, most extreme long shots are shot outdoors using daylight, making the use of artificial lighting very rare. This does not mean that you will have no control over the lighting, however; careful planning (by monitoring weather forecasts, and using software that lets you predict the length and position of shadows at any time of the year anywhere) and location scouting can let you decide how the shot will be lit to convey something meaningful about the location. An example of this can be seen in Zhang Yimou's *Raise the Red Lantern* (1991, in the emblematic shot chapter), where thoughtful scheduling allowed the shot to be taken at magic hour, taking full advantage of the unique quality of daylight during this time, thus adding beauty and poignancy to that moment in the scene.

breaking the rules

In this extreme long shot from Im Kwon-taek's Seopyeonje (1993), Dong-Ho (Kim Kyu-chul) takes a last look at his sister Song-hwa (Oh Jung-hae) before running away from the cruel man who raised them after their parents died, an itinerant singer of Pansori (a traditional Korean style of music akin to American Blues). Instead of underlining this dramatic moment in the story with close ups of the brother and sister, Im uses extreme long shots to emphasize the vast space already in place between them, foreshadowing a separation that will last years. Note that while most of the guidelines for extreme long shots were observed, the horizon was purposely placed high in the frame, against the rule of thirds. While the composition lacks the harmony and balance the rule would offer, it intelligently exploits the resulting disharmony and unbalance it creates to emphasize the abruptness and anguish felt by the characters because of their separation.

The Graduate. *Mike Nichols, 1967.*

over the shoulder shot

These shots are widely used whenever an exchange between two or more characters takes place, or when a character is looking at something. The name refers to the placement of the camera directly behind the shoulder of one of the characters, partially obstructing the frame, while the principal character faces the lens (other body parts, like hips and shoulders can also be used). The inclusion of the character with his back to the camera creates depth in the frame by adding a foreground layer to the main character and background planes. The O.T.S. shot, also known as a dirty single, is normally accomplished using **medium shots**, **medium close ups**, or **close ups** (although wider shots can be used). In cases of a dialogue exchange, the composition is designed to make the character facing the camera the focal point. Like the close up, this shot usually has a **shallow depth of field**, due to the very short camera to subject distance used to frame it. In most cases, the O.T.S. shot is edited in a matched pair, with a corresponding O.T.S. shot framed from a reverse angle. Composition, focal length, and depth of field are also usually matched, and the camera is almost always placed according to the **180° rule**.

The arrangement of visual elements in this shot lends itself to many variations that can effectively convey meaningful narrative points to the audience. The amount of space taken up by the character with his back to the camera, for instance, can make a strong statement about the power dynamics in a scene, as seen in Mike Nichols' *The Graduate* (1967), where Mrs. Robinson's shoulder takes up so much room that it visually constricts an already uncomfortable-looking Ben while she tries to seduce him (also a perfect example of **Hitchcock's rule** in action). The reverse shot does not match the composition of this example, and has a more conventional O.T.S. shot framing that firmly establishes Mrs. Robinson's dominance and Ben's vulnerability in this scene. The O.T.S. shot can also be used to manipulate the level of identification an audience has with a character, by controlling the angle at which the camera records him or her; the more it matches the point of view of the character in the foreground, the greater the audience's emotional connection and identification with the main character will be. In our example from *The Graduate*, the camera was positioned so that when Ben discovers a naked Mrs. Robinson in front of him, he is almost looking directly into the camera. This angle provides one of the highest levels of audience identification possible, letting them fully sympathize with his plight and making his reaction feel more uncomfortable than if it was shown in a profile shot, for instance. Sometimes, these key moments in the story are also emphasized by purposely not matching the composition of an O.T.S. shot and using a single for a reverse instead (without the inclusion of the character with his back to the camera). Although the O.T.S. shot is ubiquitous, it should not be thought of as just a generic or utilitarian convention; like all shots, it has the ability to make powerful narrative statements if used thoughtfully and consistently.

In this over the shoulder shot from Mike Nichols' The Graduate (1967), the composition effectively conveys how uncomfortable and overwhelmed Benjamin (Dustin Hoffman) feels when he is seduced by a naked Mrs. Robinson (Anne Bancroft), the wife of his father's business partner.

why it works

O.T.S. shots can be very effective to set up the power dynamics between two or more characters. The O.T.S. shot used in this first meeting between Red (Morgan Freeman) and Andy (Tim Robbins) in Frank Darabont's *The Shawshank Redemption* (1994) firmly establishes the foundation of their emerging friendship. The reverse shot matches this O.T.S. shot in terms of general composition, angle, focal length, and depth of field. Note how the camera was placed at an angle that is close enough to Red's line of sight so that the audience can identify with him (and with Andy in the reverse shot) but not too close, since this is their first encounter. The use of a medium close up (instead of a medium shot) also reinforces the idea that a special connection is being developed between these two characters, as does the use of shallow depth of field that effectively separates their exchange from the activity in the background.

This character's placement within the frame follows the rule of thirds, giving him proper looking room and headroom for the size of this shot. He is also framed within the frame by the inclusion of the shoulder of the character in the foreground, leading the audience's gaze toward him and making him the focal point of this composition. The angle at which the camera was placed is close to the eyeline of the character facing the camera, prompting the audience to identify with him.

This character was also placed over a sweet spot according to the rule of thirds. Note how the top of his head is cropped, since he is larger in the frame than the main character. Depth of field was controlled so that he is not as soft as the background, making him a part of the action even though he is not the focal point of this composition.

Over the shoulder shots usually include only a small portion of the subject in the foreground. This character, however, is almost completely in the frame, making him an integral part of the composition and underlining the physical proximity (and psychological closeness) that exists with the main subject of the shot.

Over the shoulder shots almost always have at least three layers of depth: foreground, middle ground, and background. The inclusion of this character in the foreground adds depth to the frame by providing an overlapping object cue along the z axis of the frame.

The shallow depth of field blurs the background, letting the audience concentrate on the facial expressions of the main character. The short camera to subject distance normally used in this type of shot might not be enough to achieve this shallow depth of field on a sunny day, so having ND filtration handy to use wider apertures is always a good idea.

Shooting with available light is no excuse for flat, boring lighting. In this shot, sunlight comes from behind the main character, creating a nice "rim lighting" effect. The reverse O.T.S. shot (right), taken by placing the camera according to the 180° rule, matches everything...including the sunlight coming from behind the main character, an impossibility unless the shots were taken at completely different times of the day or their position was cheated. Very few (if any) members of the audience will ever notice lighting manipulations of this kind as long as the shot is visually pleasing and the context of the scene dramatically compelling.

technical considerations

lenses

O.T.S. shots can be taken with **wide angle**, **normal**, and **telephoto lenses**, depending on the size of the shot, the desired **camera to subject distance**, and the apparent distance you want to create between the main and the foreground subjects. In its more conventional form, this shot is taken with a normal lens, with the camera placed right behind one of the subjects, resulting in a very short camera to subject distance and **shallow depth of field** both in the foreground and the background, leaving the main subject in sharp focus. Alternatively, focal length can be chosen to exaggerate the **z axis** distance between subjects (by using a wide angle lens) or to bring them closer together (by using a telephoto). Under special circumstances, you might want both the subject in the foreground and the main subject to be in focus simultaneously, something that might not be possible if shooting indoors with artificial light. In these cases, a **split field diopter** can be used (an attachment that effectively turns a lens into a bifocal) allowing you to focus on two planes simultaneously. Another specialized lens that can achieve this effect is the **tilt-shift lens**, which maintains focus across a diagonal, closer to the z axis instead of a plane across the **x axis**; however, its use demands a very careful staging of the action and severely restricts any movement within the shot.

format

Consumer and prosumer video cameras will make it very difficult to get the shallow depth of field this shot normally requires, because their tiny **CCD sensors** use comparatively smaller, wider lenses than their larger format equivalent (like the 2/3" CCD chips found in more expensive **HD** cameras, **16mm** and 35mm film formats). For this reason, **SD** and HD cameras should be placed as close as possible to the main subject, to minimize the camera to subject distance and get the shallowest depth of field possible. Using a wide aperture to get a shallow depth of field will be easy when shooting indoors, but shooting outdoors on a sunny day makes it a must to have **ND filtration** handy, or to engage the camera's ND switch if shooting SD or HD video. Another option would be to outfit your video camera with a **35mm lens adapter kit**, which lets you attach conventional SLR (single lens reflex) 35mm still camera lenses in front of your native lens. Since these lenses were designed for the larger 35mm format, they are comparatively longer in focal length than your native lens, and give you the same depth of field as if you were shooting with a 35mm film camera. If shooting film, it is preferable to choose slower stocks when shooting day exteriors, since they are less sensitive to light and require larger apertures, which, combined with ND filtration, will make it easier to achieve a shallow depth of field.

lighting

While changing the focal length of your lens can help you manipulate the depth of field, it will impact the composition of your shot. The more effective way to control depth of field is by manipulating the aperture, since this will allow you to keep your composition intact. However, this means that you must have control over the amount of light that reaches your CCD sensor if shooting with SD, HD, or your film stock. The shallow depth of field normally associated with **O.T.S. shots** is not difficult to achieve when shooting indoors with movie lights, since under these circumstances it is easy to use larger apertures (and you will probably have a very short camera to subject distance to help you anyway). But, shooting outdoors presents the problem of having to use smaller apertures because of the intensity of the sun, making the use of ND filtration an absolute must.

breaking the rules

The visual design of Matteo Garrone's Gomorrah (2008) includes a recurrent motif where many over the shoulder shots do not have matched reverse shots, and the focus is on the foreground, keeping the character facing the camera purposely out of focus. This deconstruction of the conventional composition and usage of the O.T.S. shot effectively adds a sense of instability and foreboding to the shady underground deals made in the film by and because of the Neapolitan-based mafia, the Camorra. In the shot above, Pasquale (left, played by Salvatore Cantalupo), an haute couture tailor, makes a deal to train Chinese garment workers who are competing against firms under Camorra protection, putting his life in extreme danger in the process.

The Shining. *Stanley Kubrick, 1980.*

establishing shot

The establishing shot is usually an exterior, **long shot** or **extreme long shot** that showcases a location where the action that follows will take place. Although these shots usually precede and contextualize scenes of action and/or dialogue, sometimes they are placed at the conclusion of a scene (that might be in an interior or exterior setting), providing a revealing or unexpected context. This simple combination of shots (exterior establishing shot followed by a dramatic scene) is a powerful cinematic convention that has been exploited by filmmakers since the early stages of film history. In the minds of the audience, a scene that immediately follows an establishing shot takes place in that location, regardless of where it is actually filmed. In most cases, scenes following establishing shots are shot at an alternate space that is more advantageous logistically and economically for the production. Establishing shots can also function as reveals, usually by following a character who arrives at a destination the audience cannot see until this wider perspective lets them see the broader location. The composition of an establishing shot must convey something about the location that communicates a particular tone, or relationship to a character, or thematic association according to the vision of the filmmaker. For this reason, not every location needs to be established; a story might have locations that are essential to the plot only because some minor action happens to take place in them, but they do not function to reveal exposition about a character or contextualize narrative content, and establishing them would unnecessarily interrupt the narrative flow. When shooting wide establishing shots outdoors in sunlight, a common mistake is to think you have little to no control over the lighting and composition to convey mood; this is not the case. Lighting can still be controlled by waiting for just the right time of the day to shoot, and composition, while more difficult to manipulate because of the size of the shot, can also be made to fit your needs by taking the time to find the right vantage point from where to shoot. A useful strategy is to develop a visual relationship between the location being established and the surrounding area included in the shot; through the careful arrangement of visual elements in the frame, a location can be made to look imposing and dominant, or innocuous and nondescript, depending on the needs of the story.

A good example of this technique is shown in a series of establishing shots of the Overlook Hotel in Stanley Kubrick's *The Shining* (1980). As the story progresses, the establishing shots slowly transform the deserted hotel from a postcard-worthy idyllic location to a desolate and uninviting place, as if slowly succumbing to the same supernatural forces that eventually drive Jack (Jack Nicholson) to want to kill his family. Regardless of where it is situated or what kind of location you need to establish, there are always ways to control the composition of a shot to communicate a particular impression about it; an essential step is to do extensive location scouting on different days and at different times of the day, so that, through scheduling, you can have as much control as possible over the look of the place you want to establish.

Stanley Kubrick uses a series of establishing shots of the Overlook Hotel throughout The Shining *(1980) that visually foreshadow Jack Torrance's (Jack Nicholson) gradual isolation from his family and eventual descent into insanity and murder.*

why it works

Alfonso Cuarón's *Children of Men* (2006) shows what happens to the world in 2027 after a virus renders all of humanity sterile. In this establishing shot, Theo (Clive Owen) arrives at the "Ark of the Arts" building, where his influential cousin Nigel (Danny Huston) works as a curator. In the dystopian future this film depicts, this building represents one of the few remnants of law and order that have managed to survive the chaos and anarchy that dominate the world. Accordingly, the composition of this shot is designed to convey its importance (by the central framing of the building in the shot), how secure it is (by including the checkpoint and armed guards in the foreground), and how cold and inhospitable it looks (by framing the building in a way that accentuates its angular, industrial features). This establishing shot successfully conveys a sense of danger and tension, two underlying recurrent features of the future shown in this film.

Horizon lines are usually placed according to the rule of thirds (either at the top or bottom third of the frame), but in this composition the horizon was placed closer to the middle of the frame, complementing the central placement of the building, and emphasizing the symmetry of the composition.

The location of this building in the frame does not follow the rule of thirds, which would require it to be placed over a sweet spot. Instead, it is centered in the frame, underlining its importance and authority as one of the remaining bastions of law and order in the otherwise chaotic world presented in this film.

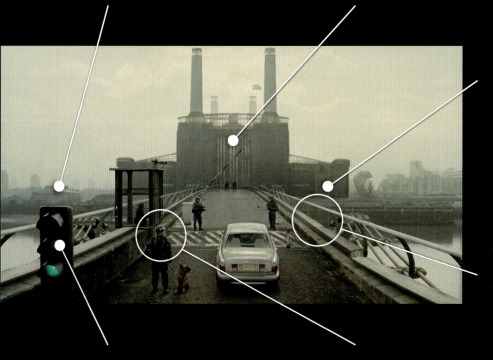

The building was shot from a vantage point that accentuates the angularity of its architecture, making it look cold and uninviting. This composition also complements the symmetric layout of the visual elements in the frame, conveying the structure's importance and authority.

The converging lines of this bridge emphasize the z axis of the frame and lead the viewer's gaze toward their vanishing point at the center of the composition, the imposing building in the background.

The inclusion of this traffic light partially protruding into the frame acts as a repoussoir, a technique designed to push the viewer's gaze toward the center of the composition. It also adds depth to the frame by implying the existence of off-screen space.

The soldiers standing along the bridge function as relative size depth cues, letting the viewer judge the long distance that exists between the car and the entrance of the building by comparing the size of the soldiers in the foreground to those in the far background.

technical considerations

lenses

The **focal length** you choose will depend on the visual features of the location you are trying to emphasize, distort, or conceal, so any type of lens might be used. You might, for instance, choose a **wide angle lens** to shoot a building from a low camera angle to exaggerate its height, making it look imposing; the same building could be shot with a **telephoto lens** at an angle that includes other buildings next to it, making it look unassuming and nondescript. If the location being established reoccurs throughout the film, you might even decide to shoot it using different focal lengths and compositions as the story progresses, to reflect changes in tone, mood, or the impact it has in the unfolding narrative and how it should be seen by the audience. **Depth of field** will be difficult to manipulate in day exteriors, since you will likely have to shoot with very small apertures from a relatively long distance (since most of the time these shots will be long or extreme long shots), even with the use of **ND filtration**. The only way to achieve shallow depth of field under these circumstances would be to use a **tilt-shift lens**, which would allow you to selectively focus on only a narrow area of your frame. Unfortunately these lenses are not available or compatible with certain formats, particularly lower-end **HD** cameras.

format

Establishing shots can contain a lot of minute visual detail in the frame. If these details are essential to the narrative, you might opt to shoot with the slowest film stock possible to reduce the amount of grain and increase the overall sharpness of the image. This is especially important if you are planning to blow up from **S16mm** to 35mm for theatrical distribution. A common practice among filmmakers, even when shooting on 35mm film stock, is to purposely overexpose the image slightly (usually by a 1/3 of an f-stop) to then pull process during the printing stage; this practice further reduces the appearance of grain while creating darker blacks. If shooting **HD** and a lot of minute visual detail is important, and if the camera supports multiple shooting modes, it would be preferable to shoot establishing shots with the highest possible resolution (1080i or 1080p rather than 720p) while also adjusting the sharpness settings to a minimum to avoid any artifacts that might degrade the quality of the image.

lighting

While it is more difficult to control lighting when shooting outdoors, it is not impossible; for instance, by consulting weather reports, you can decide to shoot on a particular day to get a certain effect. You can also use a clinometer, a device that allows you to predict the sun's position in a specific area at a given time of the year, to shoot at a time of the day when sunlight will come from a specific direction that will reveal or conceal a particular texture of your location. Shooting establishing shots at night will depend on the use of available light unless the budget is there to have large lighting instruments and the cranes/platforms needed to support them. Alternatively, the shooting of dusk for night with the time limitations it conveys is a possibility as well, especially for locations that contain light sources like illuminated windows, street lamps, and car headlights. Getting the right look to establish a specific mood will take time and patience, but it is always better to achieve the desired effect in camera, with as little manipulation as possible in postproduction. As you can see, shooting establishing shots can quickly become a complex affair, but they can be incredibly important to your story, so you should apply the same attention to detail you would use when shooting the main characters in your film. Remember, an establishing shot will conveys more than just the location where the action takes place, so make them count.

breaking the rules

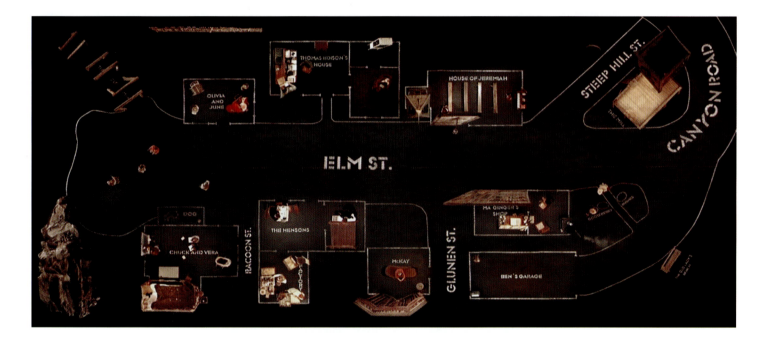

Director Lars Von Trier cleverly exploits the narrative implications of using this establishing shot to open Dogville (2003). The shot, like the rest of the movie, simultaneously adheres to and subverts the conventions associated with it; it establishes an actual, physical location (a stage with various pieces of furniture, characters, and chalk outlines) and an implied, metaphysical one (the small township of Dogville, near the Rocky Mountains) that is not present in the shot and needs to be imagined by the audience to follow the story. This rare filmic example of Brecht's "distancing effect" is meant to prevent audiences from getting emotionally involved with the story, making them more consciously critical of the events in the narrative instead.

The Silence of the Lambs. *Jonathan Demme, 1991.*

subjective shot

The subjective shot is unique in its ability to let audiences experience the action as if seen directly through the eyes of a character. The evolution of cinematic language developed a number of conventions designed to allow audiences to identify with the emotional and/or psychological state of mind of a character (through the use of P.O.V. shots, dream and fantasy sequences, and reaction shots, for instance), but none of them operates by allowing the audience to become a surrogate for a character, watching events unfold as if through their eyes, and making them an intrinsic part of the story for the length of a shot. Subjective shots accomplish this through compositions, staging of the action, and image manipulation designed to mimic the subjective point of view of a given character. The composition of a subjective shot can be carefully manipulated to match both the physical attributes of the character's perspective, and their emotional and psychological subjectivity. One of the most striking features of the subjective shot is the way it lets the other characters interact directly with the audience, by looking into the lens, speaking to, and sometimes even having physical contact with it. This interaction can be extremely powerful but also potentially very jarring to audiences, who are accustomed to experience the action from the safety of a third person perspective, as invisible and unacknowledged observers. If subjective shots are used for extended periods of time, there is a danger that audiences will find it difficult to identify with the character whose subjectivity they are experiencing, gradually disconnecting with the story. This disconnection is caused by the lack of reaction shots which ordinarily reveal the emotional response of a character. Without the ability to look a character in the eye, audiences are left uncertain as to how they should feel and react to the events they experi-ence, leading to ambiguities that fail to produce a sense of narrative clarity. The subjective shot should therefore only be used under very special circumstances and even then only for short periods of time, particularly when placing the audience in the shoes of a character will amplify the dramatic impact of a scene, or when letting them see the action through the eyes of a character provides them with a unique insight that would not be possible to experience with any other type of shot. The composition and look of the subjective shot will depend on the visual metaphor being used to show a given psychological or physical subjectivity; for instance, what would the subjectivity be of a character who suffered a stroke? What would the world look like through their eyes?

Jonathan Demme uses subjective shots in this way in *The Silence of the Lambs* (1991), at important moments in the narrative when Clarice Starling (Jodie Foster) has meaningful exchanges with Dr. Hannibal Lecter (Anthony Hopkins) and other key characters. In the example on the left, Lecter is shown unbearably close to her (and the audience), even though it was established he is in fact several feet away in previous shots from the same scene; the subjective shot visualizes just how imposing and menacing he comes across when he incisively forces Clarice to reveal an important childhood memory.

Several key scenes in Jonathan Demme's The Silence of the Lambs *(1991) have characters addressing Clarice Starling (Jodie Foster) by looking directly into the lens. This use of subjective shots allows the audience to feel what it is like to stand face to face with the menacing Dr. Hannibal Lecter (Anthony Hopkins).*

subjective shot

why it works

The subjective shot is unique in its ability to let the audience experience action through the perspective of a character. In this type of shot, characters interact with the camera as if it were an individual, looking at, speaking to, and even touching it. The composition of this shot should reflect the angle of view from which the individual would see the action. Focal length, camera movement, composition, and other kinds of image manipulation can also be used to visualize the specific physical, emotional, and psychological attributes belonging to the specific subjectivity of a character. Julian Schnabel's

The Diving Bell and the Butterfly (2007) uses subjective shots throughout most of the film to make the audience experience what life was like for Jean-Do (Mathieu Almaric) after suffering a massive stroke at age 42. The relatively few reaction shots used are complemented with a voice over from his still intact consciousness, letting audiences sympathize with his plight. Shot compositions were designed to simulate the subjectivity of the stroke victim, as seen in this example when his wife Céline (Emmanuelle Seigner) visits him.

In a subjective shot, characters interact with the camera as if it were just another character, looking directly into the lens, speaking to it, and even touching it. This kind of interaction is seldom used, but can be an extremely effective way to let audiences experience the story as if they were an integral part of it.

Although the subject leans into a static frame from off-screen, she is still given the proper amount of headroom for a shot this size. There are, however, many instances in this film where subjects are not framed according to compositional guidelines, but this is consistent with the character's subjectivity being replicated, whose paralysis prevented the use of any character-motivated camera movement.

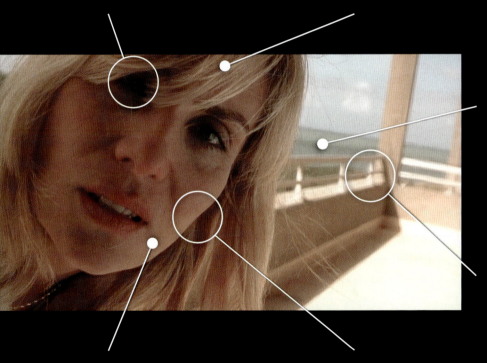

The horizon has been purposely framed askew, simulating the subjective view of the character, whose head was left drooping after his stroke. The canted angle also suggests the chaotic new reality he faces every day because of his injury. Manipulating the image to reflect the physical, emotional, and psychological state of mind of a character is a common strategy when using a subjective shot.

The very shallow depth of field is also meant to recreate the subject's impaired vision after losing sight in one eye due to the stroke he suffered. The film uses several techniques to distort the image to various degrees, reflecting the different stages of his recovery.

The slight distortion on her face and the converging perspective seen in the background indicate the use of a lens with a shorter than normal focal length, another stylistic choice designed to visualize the character's subjectivity after his stroke.

Lighting was manipulated to create a visually pleasing effect, as evidenced by the fill light providing a soft glow to this side of her face. Close ups like this one allow you to reposition or even add lights that were not present in wider shots, as long as the general look is maintained.

technical considerations

lenses

While a **normal lens** would seem like the obvious choice for a shot that simulates a character's visual perspective, this is not always the case. Other factors should be considered, like whether the shot will include camera movement (a common subjective shot technique), and what kind of camera movement will be used. For instance, if you want to conceal camera shake, **wide angle lenses** would be preferable; if the movement will be accomplished with the use of a **tracking**, **dolly**, or **Steadicam** rig, longer **focal lengths** could also be used. Lenses could also be selected to communicate a specific visual metaphor that might convey the physical, emotional, and/or psychological characteristics of the subjectivity being shown. You could use a **tilt-shift lens** to simulate the subjectivity of a character with poor eyesight, or a **telephoto** lens that narrows the **field of view** to indicate that a character is fixated with a particular object or subject. While some conventions are more established than others (like using a "fish eye" lens to show that someone is under the influence of drugs, or a double exposure to show a character is drunk), remember that every film creates its own visual vocabulary to some extent, so feel free to come up with your own visual metaphor.

format

Subjective shots often include camera movement. Usually, a handheld camera will be used, to differentiate it from the steadiness of a dolly shot and to more closely simulate the movement of a real person (although many films also use tracking and Steadicam rigs for subjective shots). If this is the case, smaller, lighter cameras would be preferable, possibly even mixing formats (for instance, if the shooting format is 35mm, one could shoot the subjective shot sequences in **Super 16mm** with a slow stock for a **35mm blow up**, or even shoot on **HD** to then upscale the footage to 2K and later

transfer to 35mm). The complexity of the camera movement and the requirements of the visual strategy devised to simulate the subjectivity will ultimately dictate the kind of hardware necessary to create the shot; no film exemplifies this better than Aleksandr Sokurov's *Russian Ark* (2002), a film shot with an HD camera on a Steadicam rig for its 91-minute single-take subjective sequence shot which travels through the Hermitage museum and 300 years of Russian history (included in the sequence shot chapter).

lighting

If the subjective shot includes camera movement, the placement of lights will have to take this into account; the moving camera creates a dynamic frame that can restrict where lights can be placed without being seen, and in many cases you might not be able to use any conventional movie lights, particularly when shooting night interiors. In these cases, a good strategy is to use practicals (sources of light that are visible within the shot and are part of the art direction for a given location, like table lamps), relamped with higher-wattage bulbs that are commonly connected to dimmer boards to control their output, providing you with enough exposure to shoot. A drawback when using this lighting strategy is that, depending on how much is seen within the shot, you might end up needing quite a few practicals. When shooting day interiors, one option is to light the location using larger fixtures strategically positioned outside windows to provide motivated lighting, freeing the camera to move almost anywhere; you can save yourself a lot of trouble and extra expense by choosing a location that is on the ground level, so that you will not have to rent cranes or extendable platforms to raise lights to a second or third story set of windows. Night exteriors are usually handled by shooting dusk for night, choosing a location that happens to have a lot of available light, or the more expensive route, by using large lighting instruments on platforms or hung from cranes.

breaking the rules

Spike Jonze's wonderfully surreal Being John Malkovich (1999) uses vignetted subjective shots to visualize what it would be like to experience life through the consciousness (and not simply the perspective) of John H. Malkovich (John G. Malkovich) after a hidden portal to his mind is discovered behind a file cabinet. In this shot, a bewildered Malkovich is seduced by Maxine (Catherine Keener) while Lotte (Cameron Diaz) experiences the action from inside the portal. This particular use of the subjective shot is unique because it lets the audience experience the action through not one, but two subjectivities simultaneously, since we hear Lotte's voice over at the same time we hear Malkovich's voice. The physical interaction between the characters was achieved through the use of an ingenious camera rig worn by the director of photography.

Mystery Train. *Jim Jarmusch, 1989.*

two shot

As its name implies, the two shot includes two characters in the same composition. Two shots are usually accomplished using **medium long**, **medium**, and **medium close ups**, although any shot that features two characters can also technically be called a two shot. An extremely common use of the two shot is as a master shot for covering a conversation between two characters, either by itself or in coordination with other shots of various sizes, designed to shape the dramatic arc of the exchange. The blocking of the characters in a two shot can make a vivid narrative point about the dynamics of their relationship; this is true of any shot that includes multiple characters, like **group shots**, but it is particularly important for two shots, because having only two characters in a composition instantly suggests there is a connection between them and elicits the audience to compare and contrast them. For instance, you could use **Hitchcock's rule** to let one character occupy more space within the composition, suggesting he or she has more power, control, or assertiveness than the other. Alternatively, if the two shot uses a medium or a **long shot**, the body language of your characters could also be used to suggest a particular dynamic between them. One important aspect to be aware of when using only a two shot to cover a conversation is that the audience will "edit" the scene themselves, by shifting their attention from one character to the other depending on which one is talking or any other aspect of their performance. While this might seem like a trivial distinction, it can have a serious impact in the way your audience engages with the story. When you use a combination of increasingly tighter shots to suggest something meaningful is taking place, the audience can afford to be passive, since the context of the scene is being revealed to them by the progression of the shots through ed-iting. When the composition stays constant and no editing is used, the audience has to become active, constantly searching for clues to decode the dramatic intent of the scene (what André Bazin, a seminal film theorist, called the "mise-en-scène aesthetic").

Jim Jarmusch uses this strategy in the "Far From Yokohama" segment of his film *Mystery Train* (1989). The story follows a teenage Japanese couple (Masatoshi Nagase and Youki Kudoh) as they visit historical blues and rock & roll landmarks in Memphis, Tennessee. Almost every shot in this segment is a two shot, suggesting both the deep connection that exists between them (even though they spend a large amount of their time arguing) and the shared isolation they experience as outsiders in a strange land. Because of the predominant use of two shots to tell their story, the exact nature of their relationship is revealed gradually, through their actions and performance, rather than by the strategic use of point of view shots and **close ups**.

The "Far From Yokohama" segment in Jim Jarmusch's Mystery Train *(1989) uses mostly two shots, suggesting the strong connection that exists between Jun (Masatoshi Nagase) and Mitsuko (Youki Kudoh), as they make a musical pilgrimage to Memphis, Tennessee.*

two shot

why it works

Two shots, like other shots that include multiple characters, let you establish the dynamics of a relationship, through body language, blocking, and the composition of the shot. However, because two shots only include two characters, their use tends to automatically imply that some type of narrative connection exists between them as well. This two shot from Ridley Scott's *Thelma & Louise* (1991), the story of two women who become wanted fugitives after one of them shoots and kills a would-be rapist, is used to establish the new relationship they have forged as a result of their journey together.

By the time this two shot is used, Louise (Susan Sarandon, left), a waitress with a damaged past who mistrusts men, and Thelma (Geena Davis, right), a mousy housewife with a controlling husband, have turned into hard core "bitches from hell" (to quote one character in the film) as they right the wrongs of the patriarchal system. Every aspect of the composition of this shot, from their body language to their placement within the frame, is designed to convey how alike their plight has made them.

A very slight low angle was used (evidenced by the fact that we can see the underside of this tin roof), emphasizing their new assertiveness and self determination at this moment in the scene. Note that it was not necessary to use an extreme low angle to achieve this effect. The subtlety of the angle allows the effect to be a complement to the rest of the compositional choices used in this shot instead of its main point.

Although characters were placed at a slight angle, they are both roughly over sweet spots created by the rule of thirds, creating a dynamic composition that gives them the proper amount of looking room. This dot marks the exact location of the top left sweet spot for the aspect ratio of this frame.

Shooting with available light will restrict your lighting options, but you can still create visually compelling images through the careful blocking of your subjects. In this two shot, the characters were positioned so that sun is behind them, creating a typical back light that separates them from the background.

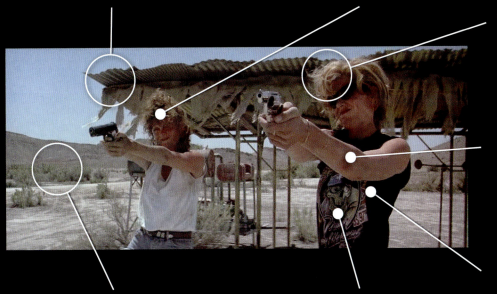

The size of this two shot lets the body language of the characters convey narrative information about them and the dynamics of their relationship. Their nearly identical stances and facial expressions are suggestive of their like-mindedness at this stage of their journey, a far cry from the very different personality traits they displayed at the beginning of the story.

Characters were placed in the frame at a slight angle, emphasizing the z axis and providing a depth cue. Their blocking also suggests that space extends beyond the boundaries of the frame, by the use of an open framing that implies the existence of off-screen space.

The deep depth of field used in this two shot makes the location an integral part of the composition and elicits audiences to establish a relationship between it and the characters. The desert location shown here is particularly important to the narrative (the first image of the film is a shot of a desert highway), because it is where a big portion of the action takes place, and because of its symbolism (emptiness, vastness, solitude, toughness, and the western genre, among others).

Thelma is slightly larger in the frame than Louise, following Hitchcock's rule; at this point in the story she has undergone a more radical change in personality than her partner, going from goofy and passive to assertive and daring (a change also suggested by her costume). She is also the focal point of this composition, resting at the end of a diagonal line that begins with Louise at the left of the frame.

technical considerations

lenses

Since two shots can come in a variety of sizes (anywhere from a **medium close up** to an **extreme long shot**), your choice of **focal length** will be determined by the specific needs of your story. Depending on the kind of relationship you want the audience to infer between the subjects, you can use a **telephoto lens** that makes it look as if the space between them along the **z axis** is shorter than in real life, or a **wide angle lens** to suggest they are farther apart. If the two shot includes a sizable portion of their surrounding area, you can also choose a focal length to affect the spatial relationships between subjects and a location. Look at the different ways characters and their environment are portrayed in the example from *Mystery Train* (at the beginning of this chapter) where only a small portion of the background is included in the frame, and the one from *Thelma & Louise* (on the previous page) where a large area surrounding them is visible in the shot. In these examples, the focal length and **camera to subject distance** were selected to manipulate the **field of view** in the composition of the shot, placing the dramatic emphasis selectively on the characters, or on both characters and location, as their narratives required.

format

The two main disadvantages of shooting with **SD** and **HD** prosumer formats instead of film (the low sensitivity of their **CCD sensors** and their general inability to produce **shallow depth of field**), are especially limiting in shots that have multiple visual elements, like two shots. While it would be possible to shoot the exact composition and depth of field seen in the *Thelma & Louise* example with almost any digital camera, only a prosumer HD camera equipped with a **35mm lens adapter kit** or a professional HD camera could replicate the framing and depth of field seen in the example from *Mystery Train*. But do not let this discourage you from incorporating the limitations of a format into the visual strategy of your film; instead, learn to exploit them and use them to your advantage.

lighting

At the very least, a two shot will include two characters and some portion of the surrounding area in the background. Commonly, characters are lit so that they stand out in the composition by making sure they are slightly brighter than anything else in the frame; with two shots, controlling how much brighter than the background they are can be used as a narrative device. If the background is kept much darker than the characters, it will be difficult to convey a relationship between the subjects and the background (as shown in the example from *Mystery Train*). Alternatively, the background can be lit so that it is perceived as being just as or even more important than the characters, underlining the relationships that might exist between them (in the example from *Thelma & Louise*, for instance, the background is as bright as they are, while the two shot from *Paris, Texas* on the opposite page features a background that is brighter than both characters). Lighting can also be used to control what elements in the frame are in and out of focus, through the manipulation of depth of field. You could ensure that the background of a two shot falls outside the area of sharp focus by using a wide aperture that produces a shallow depth of field, or ensure that it is seen clearly by using a small aperture that gives you a deep depth of field. But you cannot simply open or close the aperture without affecting the exposure of your image, so having control over the lighting becomes crucial, especially when shooting indoors (where having the extra lights necessary to use a small aperture might not be an option). Day exteriors will present you with the opposite problem; you might have too much light and need to use **ND filtration** if you want to use a large aperture to have shallow depth of field.

breaking the rules

This imaginative two shot (technically also an over the shoulder shot) from Wim Wenders' Paris, Texas (1984), brilliantly visualizes a key moment in the story, as Travis (Harry Dean Stanton), a man who deserted his family and became a drifter, reveals himself to his wife Jane (Nastassja Kinsky) at the peep show club where she works. The composition uses a one-way mirror to create a two shot that merges both characters and captures the dynamics of their relationship; Travis sees his reflection superimposed over an idealized version of the home and wife he left behind and wants to regain, but the optical illusion that lets him see his goal realized also reveals how illusory it remains, and he ultimately decides that his family is still better off without him. Because this two shot conveys so many aspects of the story by itself, it is also a great example of an emblematic shot.

City of God. *Fernando Meirelles & Kátia Lund, 2002.*

group shot

Group shots include three or more characters in the frame (with less than three characters you would have a **two shot** or a **single**); because of this, group shots are usually **medium shots**, **medium long shots**, or **long shots**, since these shot sizes are wide enough to contain multiple characters. Like other shots that include individuals and a sizable portion of their surrounding area, group shots can convey information about the dynamics of a relationship between characters or between characters and their immediate environment. For instance, the arrangement of characters in a group shot could be made to suggest disharmony and conflict between them by placing them so that no two characters face the same direction, or have the same size in the composition, or share the same space along the **x axis**. Relationships between characters and a location can be suggested by manipulating the amount of space they occupy in the frame (using **Hitchcock's rule**) to emphasize one or the other, or by using other compositional rules (like **balanced/unbalanced framings**, and **the rule of thirds**). Group shots are commonly used expositorily, at the beginning of scenes that feature dialogue between several characters, to establish their placement in a location so that tighter shots can be used later without confusing audiences about where everyone is situated. Since group shots have multiple subjects, their arrangement in a composition can also be used to emphasize the depth of a frame, by placing them along the **z axis** (providing a strong visual **depth cue** because of their diminishing **relative size**). Alternatively, placing subjects along the x axis of the frame can create a composition that is flat rather than deep. Group shots can also present you with opportunities to create compositions that are emblematic of a special moment in the story of your film, because the wider **fields of view** these shots normally require allow you to include multiple visual elements in a single frame. All of the examples included in this chapter, for instance, are both group shots and emblematic shots.

A brilliant use of a group shot occurs in Fernando Meirelles and Kátia Lund's *City of God* (2002), a film that follows the lives of two children of the favelas as they grow up; Li'l Zé (Leandro Firmino) becomes a powerful drug lord who rules over the titular favela in Rio de Janeiro, while Buscapé (Alexandre Rodrigues) strives to reach his dream of becoming a photojournalist. At a key moment in the story, Li'l Zé asks Buscapé to take a photograph of his gang after a minor victory over the police. The resulting group shot shows them standing guard over their territory, defiantly displaying their weapons as they strike a pose designed to instill fear in their enemies. The deceptively simple yet effective composition of the shot is reminiscent of a sports team photograph, with everyone lined up along the x axis of the frame (right by a shaft of light that conveniently separates them from the background). Their common body language and blocking effectively convey their unity of purpose, while their central placement and size in the frame make a powerful statement about the dynamics of their relationship with their surrounding area, the poverty-stricken favela they control.

This iconic group shot from Fernando Meirelles and Kátia Lund's City of God *(2002) perfectly visualizes the unity of purpose in Li'l Zé's (Leandro Firmino) gang and the power they wield over their favela, the ironically named "City of God."*

group shot

why it works

In addition to conveying narrative content about the relation-ships between characters and between characters and their surrounding area, the group shot's common use of framings with wider fields of view makes it ideal to create emblem-atic compositions, visualizing an important concept and/or a recurring theme at key moments in the story. In this group shot from Johnny To's *Exiled* (2006), a tension-filled gangster drama that follows two sets of hitmen from rival gangs as they thwart each other's plans, the placement of characters in the frame is designed to create suspense while establish-ing the spatial relationships between them in preparation for the dramatic shoot out that follows. Every compositional choice in this shot visualizes the conflict that exists between the characters: foreground vs. background, large vs. small, lit vs. silhouetted, and concealed vs. exposed, among others.

The wide field of view needed to include all the characters in the frame was accomplished through the use of a wide angle lens, evidenced by the visible warping of vertical lines toward the edges of the frame. The use of this lens also exaggerates distances along the z axis of the frame, adding depth to the composition.

This subject (an underground doctor being visited by both teams of hitmen to take care of their wounded) is the focal point of the composition; he occupies the brightest area in the background of the frame, and the body language of the rest of the characters leads the audience's attention toward him.

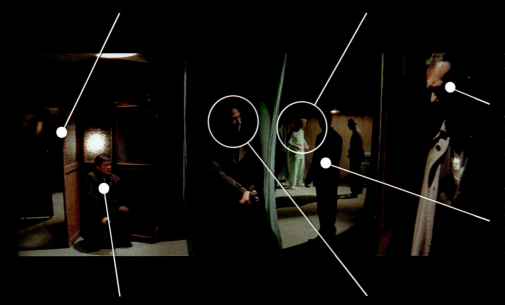

This subject, partially cropped by the edge of the frame, acts as a repoussoir (an object designed to lead the viewer's gaze to the focal point of a composition) that also implies the existence of space beyond the boundaries of the frame. He also provides a visual cue that adds depth to the frame by letting the audience compare his relative size with the characters in the middle ground and the background of the composition.

The silhouetting of these characters makes them stand out against the bright background. Within the lighting scheme used in this shot, the silhouetting also sets them up as visual opposites of the characters in the foreground, emphasizing the conflict that exists between them.

The wide framing of this group shot lets some subjects be shown in their entirety, allowing body language to add dramatic content to the scene. Note the added tension and suspense provided by the postures of the three subjects in the foreground, poised as if ready to engage in a gun battle at a

The use of pools of light surrounded by areas of complete darkness, highlighting every layer in the composition, adds contrast and depth to the frame. The low-key lighting also makes the location look foreboding and isolates each character, making it plausible for many individuals to remain hidden in

technical considerations

lenses

Since group shots can convey relationships between characters and between characters and their surrounding area, choosing a **focal length** that supports the kind of relationship you want to imply to your audience is critical. For instance, you can use a **wide angle lens** to exaggerate the distances along the **z axis** of the frame, also increasing the apparent distance between characters if they are placed at different planes in the composition (as in the example from Johnnie To's *Exiled* on the previous page). Alternatively, you could use a **telephoto lens** to compress distances along the z axis instead, creating the appearance that characters are closer than they really are, or to imply a special connection between a character in the foreground and a meaningful detail in the background of the frame (as seen in the example from Mike Leigh's *Naked*, in the medium shot chapter). If the group shot is taken in a real-life indoor location and not a movie set, be aware that the lack of space and removable walls will very likely narrow your options as to what focal length you can use, depending on the size of the shot you want (this is especially true if you want to have a **long shot**, **medium long shot**, or a **medium shot**).

format

Shooting with **SD** or **HD** formats will restrict your options to manipulate the surrounding area in group shots that have wide fields of view. Since the native lenses in these formats have generally short focal lengths, creating a composition that isolates the subjects from the background with the use of **shallow depth of field** will be much more difficult (a good example of this technique is shown in Cox's *Sid and Nancy*, in the long shot chapter). Tighter framings that bring the camera closer to the subjects are an option, but only when shooting with video formats that have larger **CCD sensors**, like those found in some prosumer and high-end HD cameras.

The use of **35mm lens adapter kits** available for some prosumer HD formats can give you much more flexibility, provided you are equipped with a good selection of 35mm lenses. The frame sizes of **16mm** and **Super 16mm** film formats, while larger than most video SD and HD CCD sensors, will still make it difficult to achieve shallow depth of field unless shorter **camera to subject distances** are used. The 35mm format is your only option if the group shot is a long shot that needs to have both a wide framing and shallow depth of field.

lighting

When group shots are taken indoors and cover a wide area, lighting can be used to support spatial relationships between characters or between characters and a location as suggested by the composition of the frame. The group shot on the previous page, from Johnnie To's *Exiled*, is a perfect example of this; if the location had been flooded with light, leaving no corner of the room unlit, the tension and suspense of the scene would have been greatly diminished. Instead, the use of low-key lighting, with small pools of light surrounded by shadows, creates an atmosphere filled with dread and danger, complementing the dynamics between the characters established by the composition of the frame. Keep in mind, however, that the wider the shot, the more difficult it will be to find places to hide the lights from the camera (note that the lights in the foreground of the group shot from *Exiled* were placed directly above the characters). One way to overcome this problem is to use practicals to light the scene (a technique also used when a shot involves extensive camera movement). When shooting night exteriors, you will have less control over the lighting, unless you can get large lighting fixtures (and a portable generator to power them). If shooting day exteriors, you can also schedule your production to use available light in an expressive way, although this requires extensive location scouting and thorough research on your part.

breaking the rules

Because of the number of subjects they often include, group shots are commonly long shots or medium shots, making it difficult to showcase facial expressions to convey dramatic content; however, this group shot of civil servants from Terry Gilliam's Brazil (1985), a film about a dystopian future where bureaucrats control every aspect of society, uses an uncharacteristic medium close up that does just that. The imposing, low-angle composition has characters placed so that they fill every available space in the bottom half of the frame, blocked in such a way to convey the oppressiveness and inflexibility of the Department of Information Retrieval, a branch of the government in charge of, among other things, the torture of suspected terrorists.

Apocalypto. *Mel Gibson, 2006.*

canted shot

Canted shots are composed with a camera tilted laterally, so that the horizon is not level and vertical lines run diagonally across the frame. The resulting compositions can create spatial imbalance or disorientation which can convey a sense of dramatic tension, psychological instability, confusion, madness, or drug-induced psychosis. Canted shots were originally introduced to the grammar of film in the 1930s, in German expressionistic films that used them to externalize the inner turmoil or deranged state of a character's psyche. The shot was also known as a "Deutsch angle" ("Deutsch" is the word for "German" in German) shot, which over time was confused and changed into today's "dutch angle" shot, even though its historic roots have no connection with the cinema of the Netherlands. Although canted shots are commonly used to represent a character's altered or abnormal state of mind, they can also be used to represent the collective psychology of a group, usually when they are experiencing a stressful or unusual situation. Another common use of the canted shot is to convey that an unnatural or abnormal situation is taking place, without necessarily reflecting a character's psychology. The degree to which the frame is canted is normally interpreted as reflecting the level of abnormality, disorientation, or uneasiness being conveyed. Extremely canted shots, with the camera tilted close to 45 degrees, are very jarring to audiences and are therefore reserved for extreme situations; conversely, tilting the camera only a few degrees can introduce a sense of underlying instability to a scene without being too distracting. Because canted shots can be very overt and noticeable to audiences, it is common to restrict their use to only a few or even just a single shot within a scene. However, if the canted angle is not too great, sometimes entire scenes are shot using them. Like all other compositional manipulations, the effect of the canted shot is lost if used too often. Two rare examples of an extensive use of canted shots include Carol Reed's *The Third Man* (1949), and Hal Hartley's *Fay Grim* (2006).

An example of a canted shot used to convey a collective altered state of mind can be seen in Mel Gibson's *Apocalypto* (2006). Set during the decline of the Mayan civilization, it follows the story of a Mesoamerican tribesman, Jaguar Paw (Rudy Youngblood), after he is abducted and taken to a large Mayan city. As he is being prepared for ritual sacrifice, a Solar eclipse takes place; the Mayan population, believing the eclipse to be an evil omen, break into a panic and beg a high priest (who obviously understands the true nature of the celestial phenomenon) to bring the sun back. At this point Gibson uses a canted shot of a group of Mayan citizens to convey their collective hysteria, visualizing their belief that the natural order of the world has suddenly gone out of balance, a mindset reflected by the high degree of inclination used in the composition of this shot.

A canted shot is used to convey the collective hysteria of the Mayan population as they experience a Solar eclipse in Mel Gibson's Apocalypto *(2006).*

canted shot

why it works

In addition to conveying a character's altered state of mind, canted shots can also amplify the tension of a dramatic moment, especially when something unsettling or abnormal is taking place in a scene, as seen in this example from John McTiernan's *Die Hard* (1988). After a group of mercenaries takes over a high rise building, New York cop John McClane (Bruce Willis) manages to systematically thwart their plans to steal millions from a vault. In this key scene, McClane stumbles upon Hans Gruber (Alan Rickman), the mastermind behind the mercenaries, who pretends to be one of the hostages to gain his trust. The entire scene is shot using slightly canted angles, adding tension to their exchange and signaling that something unsettling is taking place. As the scene continues, it is revealed that McClane suspected Gruber's true identity all along, and only pretended to trust him to pump him for information.

The lighting from below used on this character gives him a sinister, menacing look that is amplified by the inclusion of the large looming shadow behind him.

The excessive amount of headroom given to this character is motivated by the need to include the distorted shadow of his head on the wall behind him (itself canted against the angle of the canted shot), a visual cue that hints at his duplicitous nature.

Including this character in the foreground adds depth and leads the viewer's gaze to the character in the middle ground, the focal point of the composition in this over the shoulder shot.

The relatively wide framing (somewhere between a medium shot and a medium close up) allowed the inclusion of several vertical lines from the mise en scène, making the slight inclination of this canted shot very apparent.

Using a wide angle lens extends distances along the z axis of the frame (note the apparent wide space between the two characters even though they are only at arm's length of each other), and also adds some distortion to the frame that complements the awkwardness suggested by the skew of the angle.

The camera to subject distance and large aperture combination resulted in a slightly shallow depth of field, keeping only the main subject in the middle ground, the focal point of this composition, in sharp focus.

technical considerations

lenses

The effect of a canted shot can be augmented or minimized depending on the **focal length** used. Since canted shots are made apparent by the inclination of vertical lines present in the frame, it is important to create compositions that include them prominently; this is especially important if the canted angle is very slight and the framing is tight enough to exclude most of the surrounding area. This is where your choice of focal length can make a difference. Depending on the details of your scene, using a **wide angle lens** that extends distances along the **z axis** can make verticals in the background of your frame less apparent than if you were using a **telephoto lens** that would bring them closer to the foreground (since a telephoto compresses distances along the z axis). However, manipulating the focal length alone is not enough if other aspects of your composition, including **depth of field**, lighting, and art direction, are not also taken into account. For instance, in the example from Gibson's *Apocalypto* at the beginning of this chapter, a telephoto lens was used to compress space along the z axis of the frame, not to make the canted shot more apparent (since it already uses a very inclined angle), but to compress the Mayan citizens into a unified mass, visually conveying their shared collective mindset as they witness a Solar eclipse. On the other hand, the wide angle lens used in the example from McTiernan's *Die Hard*, on the previous page, added optical distortion to the composition; combined with lighting and blocking choices, the added distortion emphasizes the unsettling tone suggested by the use of the only slightly canted shot.

equipment

Most tripods will let you loosen their head mounts, allowing you to tilt the camera to create a slightly canted shot without the need to adjust the legs. If a more canted angle is desired, you can extend one of the tripod legs longer than the other two, or even attach the base plate that holds the camera to the tripod sideways, so that its tilting action will slant the camera laterally. Regardless of the method you choose to create a canted shot, keep in mind that any adjustment that renders the camera unbalanced requires extra measures to prevent the tripod from tipping over.

lighting

Any manipulation of the depth of field will involve controlling the amount of light reaching the film or **CCD sensor**. In the example from *Apocalypto*, a telephoto lens was combined with a relatively small aperture to ensure that as many individuals as possible included in the canted shot were in focus, even though the eclipse effect (a combination of a live effect with digital tweaking during postproduction) reduced the amount of available light; this was accomplished thanks to the high sensitivity of the Panavision Genesis (a high end **HD** camera) used to shoot this movie. A smaller aperture could also have been used in the example from *Die Hard*, without sacrificing the low-key lighting used to add an ominous mood to the scene, simply by increasing the output of the lights used on the set. While a smaller aperture would have produced a sharp background that would have made the verticals in that area of the frame more apparent, it would have also potentially taken attention away from the main subject of the composition, breaking one of the rules for **over the shoulder shots**.

breaking the rules

Since canted shots already suggest an altered or uneasy situation, it is unusual to see them combined with disorienting camera moves. However, a key moment in Peter Weir's The Truman Show (2002) is underlined by the use of a canted shot that is imaginatively complemented with a dynamic camera attached to a revolving door, conveying Truman Burbank's (Jim Carrey) unsettling realization that things are not what they seem in his idyllic hometown.

Being There. *Hal Ashby, 1979.*

emblematic shot

Emblematic shots have the power to communicate abstract, complex, and associative ideas with compositions that reveal special connections between visual elements in the frame. Emblematic shots can "tell a story" with a single image, conveying ideas that are generally greater than the sum of their parts. Audiences watching Luke Skywalker looking at the twin suns of Tatooine in George Lucas' *Star Wars* (1977), get more out of that shot than the literal content of the image (young man watches suns setting). Instead, the audience is encouraged to identify larger meanings from the connections and associations contained in the visual elements, specifically by their placement in the composition and the symbolism associated with certain images. These connections transform the concrete meaning "young man watches suns setting" into the symbolic "he feels his future is out of reach" in the minds of the audience. There are many different approaches to create these shots, but the first step is to have a clear understanding of the themes, subtexts, and core ideas in your story; once these are identified, you can design compositions that support them visually. You could, for instance, use **Hitchcock's rule** to create a composition that emphasizes a particular visual element over another, or use any of the compositional principles (like **balanced/ unbalanced** framings, the **rule of thirds**, etc.) to establish a specific relationship between visual elements in the minds of the audience. Emblematic shots are usually placed at the beginning or at the end of particularly meaningful scenes or sequences. When used at the beginning of a scene, they tend to set up the tone of what follows. When they appear at the end of a scene or sequence, they tend to comment on, or contextualize, the events that led to the emblematic shot. Another common practice is to reuse or recreate an em-

blematic shot toward the end of a film, alerting the audience that a story has come full circle and that the ending is near (a popular technique in **image systems**). When creating an emblematic shot, think about the meaning being implied by the arrangement of subjects in the shot. Is your composition supporting what is taking place in the scene/sequence/film? Challenging it? Foreshadowing an event that will take place later? Commenting on issues that are not directly related to the plot but are ultimately what your film is really about? Can you take your emblematic shot out of the film, show it to someone who doesn't know the story, and have him or her recognize what your film is about?

Hal Ashby's *Being There* (1979) uses an emblematic shot early in the film, right after its protagonist, an idiot savant named Chance (Peter Sellers), finds himself homeless in Washington, D.C. after the death of his employer. The composition of the shot cleverly suggests Chance's eventual ascendancy to the presidency of the United States (symbolically represented by the Capitol building and the green traffic light giving him the "go ahead"), while the isolated path he walks on is suggestive of his unique look at life. This simple, yet effective emblematic shot introduces and foreshadows themes that are explored throughout the film.

In Hal Ashby's Being There *(1979), Chance the Gardener (Peter Sellers) finds himself homeless and roaming the streets after his benefactor suddenly dies; the inspired composition of this early shot in the film cleverly foreshadows his ultimate destination: the Presidency of the United States of America.*

emblematic shot

why it works

Emblematic shots are not easy to conceive, but they can be very effective at communicating complex, non-verbal, or associative information. In these shots, the director's take on the themes explored in the film are visualized, through the thoughtful arrangement of visual elements within the frame. A common approach to the composition of these shots is to use Hitchcock's rule, organizing the visual elements in a way that lets audiences create meaningful connections to the story. In this emblematic shot from Zhang Yimou's *Raise the Red Lantern (1991)*, Songliang (Gong Li), a girl married

against her will to a rich man who already has several wives, has a chance encounter with one of her stepsons, Feipu (Chu Xiao). Although they meet only briefly, this is the first time she has a meaningful emotional connection with a man since her arranged marriage, because traditional "house rules" severely restrict her every move. Appropriately, their last gaze of each other is visually obstructed by a section of her husband's house, framed to present a formidable obstacle between them, both physical and symbolic.

This character was purposely placed against an empty background, making her quite noticeable even though she occupies very little room in the frame and the composition is visually dense.

Following Hithcock's rule, the structure between the characters dominates the composition of the shot, both because of its size and its centralized placement in the frame. Note that by cropping the top of the structure, a visual cue is created that suggests it cannot be fully contained within the boundaries of the frame, further emphasizing its size and importance.

This character is dwarfed by the lavish surround-ings of the opulent house (of which this is only the rooftop!), underlining his lower status within the family. Note that although small in the frame, he is made to effectively stand out by silhouetting him against the bright background, a good idea given the visual complexity of this shot.

Note how everything in the frame, from the fore-ground to the background, is in sharp focus. Using a deep depth of field lets the audience notice the spatial and size relationships between the char-acters and their surroundings; a shallow depth of field would not have allowed this visual statement.

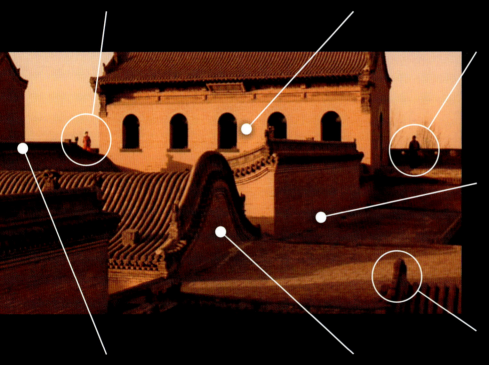

This small adornment, partially protruding into the composition, adds depth by implying the existence of off-screen space. This technique is designed to overcome the inherent flatness of the frame.

The horizon was placed close to the top third of the frame according to the rule of thirds, provid-ing more room to crowd the rest of the frame with the various structures that comprise the elaborate roof of this house (following Hitchcock's rule). The extra room taken by the house also creates a sense

These structures in the foreground and middle ground add depth to the composition by empha-sizing the z axis of the frame. They also lead the viewer's gaze to the silhouetted character in the background.

technical considerations

lenses

Since the emblematic shot relies on viewers making connections between visual elements in the frame, the use of smaller apertures to obtain **deep depth of fields** (to ensure everything is in focus) is common. While using smaller apertures is not difficult when shooting outdoors on a sunny day (where you will have more light than you need), you will have to have plenty of lights when shooting indoors. If you're shooting film, there are ways to make it easier to achieve a deep depth of field indoors, by choosing the right film stock (see below). Another technique to get a deep depth of field is to choose a lens with a short focal length, which will produce the appearance of one, but you will have to take into account the distortion it creates and the radical change in the **field of view** your composition will have. Another option would be to use a specialized lens like a **split field diopter**, which lets you have both background and foreground subjects in focus simultaneously, with the caveat you will also have an area of blurriness in the middle of the composition (where the join between the two lenses is located). You could also use a **tilt-shift lens**, which allows you to have a plane of focus along a diagonal toward the **z axis**, but this will require the careful arrangement of visual elements only along this axis, severely restricting your compositional choices.

format

The smaller apertures needed to get a deep depth of field let less light through, necessitating the use of extra lighting to compensate when shooting indoors. Choosing a fast film stock in this situation will make it possible to use a smaller aperture, since they require less light to record an image than slower stocks. You could also try to increase the **camera to subject distance** to create a deeper depth of field, but this is not always an option when shooting indoors because of space restrictions. Shooting on **SD** or **HD** works in your favor in this case; the smaller **CCD sensors** most consumer and prosumer cameras use make it very easy to achieve a deep depth of field, since their lenses have to produce a much smaller image and therefore have much shorter **focal lengths** than their larger format counterparts.

lighting

One of the ways that emblematic shots are identified as such, is through a lighting scheme that is slightly different from the rest of the film, creating a greater impact and demanding extra attention form the viewer. The first two examples used in this chapter exemplify this special attention to lighting. In the example on the previous page, the natural light used in the scene produces very long shadows. The director shot this scene either very early in the morning or very late in the afternoon, obtaining a beautiful orange glow. Shooting during or close to magic hour can produce amazing results, but dramatically reduces the amount of time you have to shoot. Faster film stocks will make it possible for you to continue shooting right up until the sun sets if shooting at dusk, long after digital video cameras start to display video noise. The wide field of view of this shot would have made it nearly impossible to light with artificial lighting, unless cost was of no concern. Just remember that magic hour is never really an hour (but more like 20 to 30 minutes)!

breaking the rules

Although emblematic shots commonly rely on a complex arrangement of visual elements to make their point, sometimes simple compositions, coupled with clever blocking of actors and inspired casting and art direction decisions, can be just as effective. In this medium long shot from Jonathan Demme's The Silence of the Lambs (1991), Clarice Starling (Jodie Foster) enters an elevator filled with male FBI recruits, who provide a strong visual contrast because of their gender, the color of their uniforms, height, and body language. Clarice is the focal point of the composition, placed at the center of the frame, looking besieged by the males around her (especially by the two at her sides, who seem particularly annoyed by her presence). Her gaze is fixed upward (Lecter tells her that what she seeks most of all is "advancement") while her hands are clasped over her genitals, one of many visual cues in this film that underline the subtext of sexual tension between Clarice and male figures of authority.

The Soloist. *Joe Wright, 2009.*

abstract shot

The abstract shot originated in early avant-garde and experimental films from the 1920s; although initially they were used exclusively in these kinds of films, they were eventually incorporated in mainstream narrative films (a famous example being the "Stargate" sequence in *Kubrick's 2001: A Space Odyssey*). These shots emphasize colors, textures, patterns, shapes, lines, and composition over their literal content. They are usually non-representational and non-referential, making it difficult or sometimes even impossible to recognize the subject of their compositions. Because of their abstract nature, audiences tend to extract meaning from these shots based on the raw emotional connection the graphic qualities of the image suggest, not unlike the associations conjured after looking at the inkblots of a Rorschach test. Sometimes, abstract shots have a subject that is partially recognizable but is somehow distorted or abstractly presented in some way, resulting in an image that is simultaneously familiar and foreign. Abstract shots are also created by showing a fragmented aspect of a subject, isolating a visual detail in a way that makes it difficult to identify without seeing it in a wider view. Because these shots are by design visually striking, they can be especially useful as part of the **image system** of a film. These shots are commonly used to convey subtextual ideas that are not explicitly addressed, but are instead suggested by the graphic qualities of the image itself. Because of this, abstract shots can add extra layers of meaning to a narrative, sometimes commenting on the action of a scene, the intentions of a character, or simply contributing to a recurring visual theme or motif that somehow feeds into the larger canvas of your story. The length of time an abstract shot (or a group of them) is kept on the screen should be carefully planned, because their appearance normally has the effect of bringing a stop to the conventional flow of a narrative. When seeing an abstract shot, audiences have to become active rather than passive observers if they are to understand how and why that shot connects with the rest of the story; if this is done too often or for too long, there is a possibility their investment with the characters will wane, but this of course depends on how well the abstract shots are integrated into the fabric of the story.

A good example of an abstract shot occurs in Joe Wright's *The Soloist* (2009), a film that follows the relationship that develops between a journalist for the L. A. Times, Steve Lopez (Robert Downey Jr.) and Nathaniel (Jamie Foxx), a musically gifted homeless man who suffers from schizophrenia. After Lopez takes an interest in Nathaniel's well-being, he brings him to a Los Angeles Symphony Orchestra rehearsal, where we are shown a series of abstract shots of colored lights as Nathaniel listens to the music. The idea behind these shots is not that he experiences music as flashing lights, but to convey an abstract sense of his deep and complex connection with rhythm, harmony, and melody that cannot be conveyed with more literal, representational imagery.

Joe Wright's The Soloist *(2009) contains scenes that use abstract shots to visualize the subjectivity of Nathaniel, a musically gifted homeless man (Jamie Foxx), when he experiences a musical performance. The abstract shots (reminiscent of the "Stargate" sequence in Kubrick's 2001: A Space Odyssey) suggest the uniqueness of his connection to music.*

abstract shot

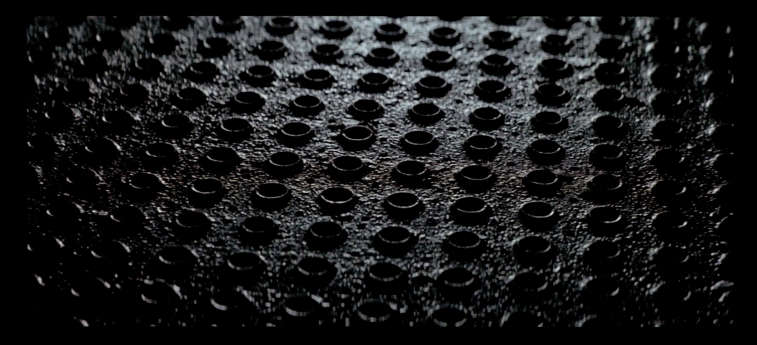

why it works

Terrence Malick's *The Thin Red Line* (1998), a poetic examination of war and its effect on the lives of the soldiers who fight it, contains several instances where the narrative takes a detour to concentrate on seemingly irrelevant visual details. These highly stylized shots usually concentrate on an aspect of the location where the action of the scene happens. In this example, the abstract shot is cut in the middle of a conversation between Witt (Jim Caviezel) and Hoke (Will Wallace) after they are caught AWOL and thrown in a brig.

As Witt ponders his future, he momentarily focuses on the subject of the shot shown above, prompting him to reminisce about his childhood. We are never shown what the subject of this shot is, but its graphic qualities can be interpreted as evoking conformity (by the repeating pattern), the inorganic (when compared to similar shots used in other scenes that showcase plants and animals), and the military (by the greenish metal texture), all recurrent motifs examined in the philosophical narrative of this film.

The same care and attention used when lighting human subjects should also be applied to objects, something beginning filmmakers often forget. In this case, lights were positioned at an angle that reveals the rough texture of the metal work, making even this abstract shot look visually interesting.

The metal grill was shot at an angle that emphasizes the z axis of the frame and suggests the existence of off-screen space to the audience, a technique commonly used to create depth and avoid the inherent two-dimensionality of the frame.

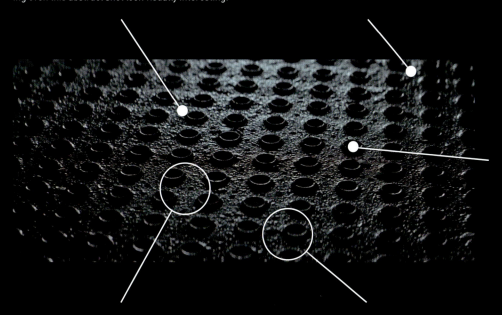

The composition of this shot prevents the audience from identifying exactly what they are looking at, by purposely avoiding any visual details that could be used for referencing either its scale or location within the scene. Because of this, a viewer can only focus on the purely graphic qualities of the shot: its patterns, textures, and colors.

Sometimes, texture cannot be properly revealed solely through lighting. Adding a liquid agent to a subject to make its texture become visually engaging is a common practice, and the reason why so many night exterior scenes feature wet streets.

The shallow depth of field focuses the audience's attention on the center of the frame, even though it is indistinct from the rest of the composition; this adds a sense of mystery and ambiguity to exactly what the audience is meant to focus on this shot, effectively underlining the abstract nature of the image.

technical considerations

lenses

Abstract shots can be created using various techniques that can include a combination of lenses, filtration, special lighting, and even post-production processes. Often, abstract shots are just **extreme close ups** that magnify a small detail (sometimes with the use of a **macro lens**) of a subject to such degree as to make it virtually unrecognizable. Another way to create abstract shots is by purposely adding some visual distortion to the subject; the easiest way to do this is by using the lens blur that happens when an object is out of focus, although specialized lenses like **split field diopters** and **tilt-shift lenses** can also be used, depending on the level of distortion desired (since these lenses allow you to selectively control the focusing range over a section of the image). Alternatively, abstract shots sometimes emphasize patterns or lines present in the subject that might have to be in focus for their associated meaning to come across. In this case, the natural distortion (or lack thereof) resulting from the use of **wide angle**, **normal**, and **telephoto** lenses should be taken into account and used accordingly.

format

Regardless of the format, any camera-oriented variable or adjustable setting is fair game to create abstract shots. The more you are familiar with the technical capabilities of your camera, the more options you will have to push the limits of the stylistic envelop. Shooting on film lets you shoot at frame rates that are slower or faster than the normal sync speed of 24 fps (25 fps in Europe), which in some cases can be used to create abstract shots. Undercranking, or shooting at frame rates slower than the norm, results in fast motion when played back at regular speed; combined with an open shutter (available only if your camera has a variable shutter function) can produce a motion blur effect, especially if the subject of the shot includes a lot of movement (like the example from

Reconstruction on the next page). If the undercranking requires even slower frame rates than those available in your camera, it is also possible to use an intervalometer (a device that lets you shoot at intervals of several seconds or even minutes per frame), but be aware that not all film cameras are equipped to be controlled this way. It is also important to remember that undercranking causes more light reach the film, especially when combined with an open shutter, so exposure compensation is essential. If shooting **HD**, the option to shoot at lower frame rates is only available in some prosumer and higher-end cameras, although it would be possible, for instance, to shoot this footage with a still digital camera as still images to then combine them by importing every frame into an editing program (laborious, but possible, especially if the shot does not need to be too lengthy in duration). Most NLE (non-linear editing) systems have all kinds of video effects that can be used to distort images, but if you shoot on film and plan to finish on film, these effects will have to be scanned from the video files you output (assuming their resolution is acceptable to you; otherwise, they will have to be recreated at a much higher resolution) and transferred to a negative so that they can be incorporated into the final cut of your film, which can be an expensive proposition.

lighting

Some abstract shots are made entirely of light patterns that can be created from scratch by the filmmaker or found "as is" at a location (for example, a commonly used abstract shot consists of out-of-focus car headlights shot at night with a telephoto lens). Lighting can also be used to distort an image by purposely adding flares, done by simply aiming lights toward the lens. If the abstract shot is meant to showcase the texture of a subject, lighting can be used to reveal or conceal it, as needed (as seen in the example on the previous page).

breaking the rules

The narrative of Christoffer Boe's Reconstruction (2003) follows the strange events that happen after Alex (Nikolaj Lie Kaas) leaves his girlfriend Simone (Maria Bonnevie) for Aimee (also played by Maria Bonnevie), seemingly causing an alternate reality to be created where none of his previous acquaintances recognizes him. The film has several abstract shots interspersed throughout the story, like the one above, an undercranked shot of a subway tunnel shown when Alex leaves his girlfriend on a train to pursue Aimee. Unlike most abstract shots, in this case we can easily recognize the source of the image, but the stylization created by shooting at a lower frame rate, combined with creative sound design, manages to make the audience concentrate on the shape, color, and texture of the image and the sci-fi concepts it evokes (a wormhole? A tunnel to an alternate universe?) rather than the actual content of the shot.

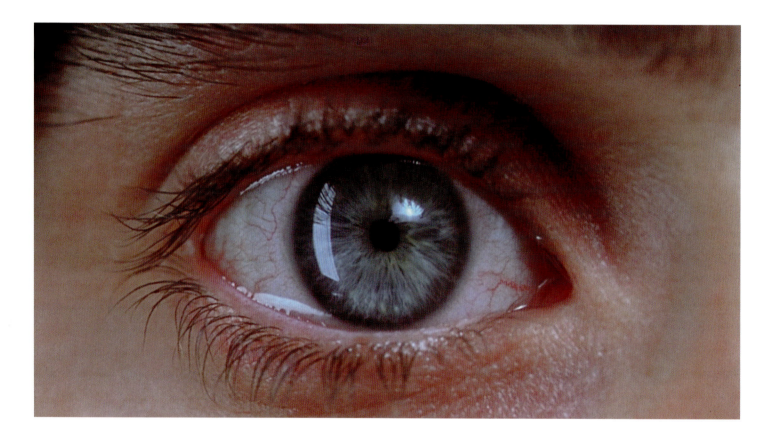

Requiem for a Dream. *Darren Aronofsky, 2000.*

macro shot

All macro shots are **extreme close ups**, but not all extreme close ups are macro shots. The difference lies in the amount of magnification of the image. For instance, while you might be able to get a very tight close up of an eye using a **prime lens**, you will not be able to get closer than the nearest **depth of field** limit for the shortest focusing distance that the lens allows, normally about 12 inches. A macro lens is a specialized lens designed to work at extremely close focusing distances, and will let you get much closer (2 inches or less), resulting in a huge image of the eye in the frame. This makes macro shots ideal to capture extremely small details of characters and objects. Like extreme close ups and **close ups**, the closeness of macro shots can add a strong visual emphasis to a subject that generates certain expectations regarding its narrative significance (as per **Hitchcock's rule**), so their use should be justified at some point in the story; for instance, a macro shot can be used to showcase an object whose importance is unknown when first presented, but is later revealed. Another common use involves editing a macro shot at the end of a series of shots of a subject that get increasingly tighter, conveying an increasing sense of tension or importance. The high level of magnification macro shots are capable of also lets you showcase textures and patterns that are so small in real life that in some cases they become completely unrecognizable to audiences when shown blown up, making them ideal for **abstract shots** that do not have a direct plot function, but are nonetheless integral to the **image system** of a film. Sometimes, the graphic qualities of a macro shot is used to generate a question in the minds of the audience, by showing them an abstract shot they can not identify at first, to then cut to a series of increasingly wider shots that finally reveal the subject. Because of their unique technical requirements, macro shots have the common feature of having an extremely shallow depth of field, which will severely restrict any movement by the subject in the frame.

Darren Aronofsky uses macro shots in his film *Requiem for a Dream* (2000) as part of mini-montages that encapsulate the experience of being under the influence of psychotropic drugs. In these visually arresting images, macro shots of pupils dilating (shot in time lapse) are combined with other extreme close ups of dollar bills, increased blood flow through a vein, various drugs in powder form being set up for consumption, and an imaginative sound design. The use of macro shots in these montages cleverly allow the filmmaker to present the audience with images that they are familiar with that look unusual because of their high degree of magnification, creating a visual metaphor for the heightened perception of a drug user's experience. Macro shots are technically difficult to accomplish, but can provide you with memorable, visually striking images with a level of detail that no other shot can show.

Darren Aronofsky's Requiem For A Dream *(2000) uses a series of recurrent macro shots of pupils dilating in highly stylized montages that visualize the effects of psychotropic drug usage. Only a macro shot is capable of capturing this high degree of magnification.*

macro shot

why it works

Macro shots capture extremely small details of a subject, revealing textures and features even an extreme close up cannot show. The closeness of this shot can make even mundane objects, actions, or details of characters visually interesting, while the emphasis it provides generates the expectation that what is shown is narratively important and meaningful to the story. An example of this is seen in Sean Penn's visually stunning *Into the Wild* (2007), a film that follows the plight of Chris McCandless (Emile Hirsch) as he struggles to survive the harsh Alaskan wilderness. Throughout the film, we see him carve extra holes into his belt as his situation worsens and he physically wastes away. With every extra hole he carves, we are shown increasingly tighter shots of the knife cutting into the leather. Appropriately, the last hole he makes takes on a monumental significance because it is shown with a macro shot, making it impossible to get any closer while conveying the impending doom that follows not too long after this shot is shown.

The blade is centered in the frame, giving it a strong visual emphasis as it cuts into the belt. Not following the rule of thirds in this case makes for a more powerful and confronting image, complementing the tension already present in the scene.

The macro shot can reveal a lot of detail that would otherwise go unnoticed, like the engravings on this belt; the added narrative emphasis is justified because this item has been a recurrent prop throughout the film, gauging the character's chances for survival.

The belt was framed so that it crosses the frame diagonally, implying the existence of off-screen space and adding depth to the shot by accentuating the z axis of the frame.

This background does not match the one seen in the preceding wider shots (shown above), but the sudden change in shot size (from a medium shot to this macro), combined with the extremely shallow depth of field, the brevity of the edit, and the highly dramatic content, make the lack of continuity imperceptible to most viewers.

The depth of field in a macro shot is extremely shallow, making it especially critical to place the most important aspect of the shot within the area of sharp focus; in this case, the tip of the blade as it digs into the leather belt.

technical considerations

lenses

The options available to create these shots will depend on your shooting format; there is a wide selection of macro lenses available for **16mm** and 35mm film, while prosumer **HD** formats have close-up lenses, diopters, and wide angle converters that attach directly to the native lens of the camera. If shooting HD with a **35mm lens adapter kit**, you will also have many macro lenses designed for still photography at your disposal. You should be aware, however, that not every lens that can be used for macro cinematography will yield the same results. Depending on the needs of your shot, especially in terms of image quality and degree of magnification, you might want to use a macro lens designed specifically for that purpose instead of the cheaper alternatives (such as close up lenses, wide angle converters, and diopters). Another benefit of using an actual macro lens is that they have barrel markings that indicate the level of magnification ("1:1," for instance, denotes that the size of the subject in the frame will match its size in real life; "1:2" means the image captured will be half the actual size, etc.) as well as the focusing distance, making exposure calculations much simpler. Since these shots involve an extremely short **camera to subject distance**, the resulting **depth of field** will invariably be so extremely shallow that is often confined to a plane instead of a region, making focusing very difficult, especially if there is even the tiniest movement by the subject. One way to alleviate this situation is by extending the depth of field through the use of smaller apertures, as explained in the next column.

format

If shooting with a prosumer **HD** camera, you should be prepared to have enough lighting to let you get deeper depths of field, since you cannot increase the sensitivity of a **CCD sensor** (unless you are willing to compromise image quality by engaging the gain mode), and you will lose a lot of light with the extra glass in front of your native lens, especially if the macro lens will be added to an existing **35mm lens adapter** kit. Less expensive, consumer-grade HD cameras have an advantage since many come with a built-in macro mode; when engaged, it allows focusing on subjects that are almost touching the lens, saving you the expense of having to rent or purchase a macro lens adapter or a wide angle converter. The downside of using these cameras is that their HD formats have a lot of compression, and in some cases are cumbersome or even impossible to edit with some NLE (non-linear editing) systems without first transcoding to a different format. Having a large preview monitor to confirm the focus of macro shots is almost a necessity, since most on-board LCD screens are simply too small for this purpose.

lighting

In some cases, the depth of field in macro shots is so shallow it cannot be measured as a range, but only as a total. Because of this, even the slightest movement from either the subject or the camera can throw an image out of focus. The only way to ameliorate this situation is to increase the depth of field as much as possible by closing down the aperture, which can only be done if additional lights are added to prevent underexposing the image. Keep in mind that even with extra lights, the resulting depth of field will still be very shallow, but even a small increase in the depth of field will make it easier to get a usable image. It is also important to remember that the closeness of the camera to the subject can result in the lens casting a shadow over the subject, restricting your placement of lighting fixtures; in this case, diffused sources of light will work best, and there are also specialized "ring lights" that can be fitted right on the lens and provide soft, diffused light that can solve this problem.

breaking the rules

The imaginative opening credit sequence in Andrew Niccol's Gattaca (1997) uses a series of macro shots of clipped fingernails, shaved hair, and dried skin flakes falling in slow motion, establishing their importance in a world where even the smallest organic trace can be used to identify people who were not genetically engineered before birth and therefore considered "invalids." Some of the shots, however, are not macros at all; large plastic props made to look like skin flakes and shot at 360 frames per second were used to simulate them instead, creating a more visually compelling image than what could have been done with a macro lens. The use of an extremely shallow depth of field makes the shot indistinguishable from the rest of the real macros used in the sequence.

The Conversation. *Francis Ford Coppola, 1974.*

zoom shot

Originally introduced to movies in the late 1950s, the zoom lens allowed, for the first time, to change a lens' **focal length** while a shot is taken, letting filmmakers have a dynamic **field of view** without the need to move the camera or switch lenses. Although zoom shots resemble **dolly shots**, they differ in the way they depict space and movement. In a zoom shot, the camera remains stationary, maintaining a constant perspective as the lens zooms from **wide angle** to **telephoto** (zoom in) or from telephoto to wide angle (zoom out). In a dolly shot, the perspective does not remain constant, because the camera itself is being moved. Unlike dolly shots, where audiences feel as if they are moving toward or away from something in the frame, zoom shots make audiences feel as if an aspect of the composition is being brought toward or away from them. The primary function of a zoom shot is to change the composition of the shot as it progresses, so that it either includes previously unseen elements, or excludes already seen aspects of the composition to concentrate on a single subject. The change in focal length can be done manually, by adjusting a zoom ring on the lens itself, or with the help of a servo motor that allows an operator to control the speed at which the focal length is changed (basically mimicking the zoom switch in a video camera). The zooming action can be smooth and steady or quick and jarring, depending on the feel you want the audience to get from the shot. A frantic and unsteady change in focal length, often used while hand holding the camera in action films, showcases the means used to adjust the composition as much as the change in composition; in this case, framing errors and quick adjustments to the shot are part of the visual language of the genre and are not seen by the audience as distracting (a legacy of the documentary tradition, which introduced quick reframes using zoom lenses to catch the action in real time). Because zoom shots can radically change the framing of a shot without having to switch lenses, they often take the form of long takes (shots that last more than the average length of just a few seconds), or edited in rapid succession to create a sense of tension and danger, depending on the speed and steadiness used to change the focal length.

A classic example of a zoom shot occurs in the opening title sequence of Francis Ford Coppola's *The Conversation* (1974), where a high angle **extreme long shot** of Union Square in San Francisco is shown while the audience hears fragments of a conversation that is obviously being secretly recorded somewhere below. The shot smoothly zooms into the square, slowly tightening the frame until it finally reveals its target: Harry Caul (Gene Hackman), a surveillance expert hired to record a conversation between a couple who might be committing adultery. The use of a slow zoom in shot, coupled with the sound of the conversation being recorded, makes the audience complicit in the act of spying, cleverly introducing one of the central themes of this film.

The opening title sequence from Francis Ford Coppola's The Conversation *(1974) marks the first use ever of an electronically controlled zoom lens in a film, with a shot that gradually reveals the central character, Harry Caul (Gene Hackman).*

zoom shot

why it works

When a zoom shot changes its focal length suddenly, it can convey a sense of urgency, tension, and danger; quick adjustments to the frame, unstable compositions, and temporarily out of focus subjects are normal and expected with this style of shooting. The overall effect for the audience is that they are witnessing action as it happens, in real time, even though most of the time this is not the case. In this example from Paul Greengrass' *The Bourne Supremacy* (2004), Jason

Bourne (Matt Damon) has just discovered that somebody has been sent after him, prompting him to pick up his girlfriend Marie (Franka Potente) to escape the threat. The shot quickly and unsteadily zooms in (or "crash zooms") from a composition that includes Marie in the foreground to a waiting Jason in the background, underlining the urgency and tension of this moment in the story.

This subject position in the frame follows the rule of thirds, creating a dynamic composition that is further emphasized by the blocking of the subjects along the z axis of the frame, creating a sense of depth. Note the correct amount of headroom for a shot this size given to the subject, also a result of using the rule of thirds.

The short camera to subject distance used in this shot resulted in a shallow depth of field, throwing the background out of focus. Since this zoom shot is changing the focal length and switching the focal point from the foreground to the background, it was necessary to rack focus as the composition was adjusted.

The composition of the shot was carefully designed to ensure the car in the background would occupy an area of the frame that is within the line of sight of the character in the foreground and the camera, yet the use of a crash zoom to execute the shot conveys the impression to the audience that this action is simply happening in real time, unrehearsed.

The placement of this subject in the frame gives him a bit too much headroom, but these small framing errors are expected with this shooting style, adding a documentary-like touch of realism that increases the drama and tension in the scene.

The inclusion of this subject's forehead is no accident. It acts as a repoussoir, an object included in the frame to lead the viewer's gaze to the focal point of the composition. It also adds depth to the frame by implying the existence of off-screen

Note the precise placement of the subject so that he is framed within the frame by the shrubbery in the foreground and the window of the car, making him stand out even though he is not in the brightest area of the composition.

technical considerations

lenses

Zoom lenses come in a variety of **zoom ratios**, giving you many **focal length** options during shooting. One thing to keep in mind is that zoom lenses have more internal elements than **prime lenses** (lenses with a fixed focal length), and are therefore slower, with a maximum aperture that will be significantly smaller than the maximum aperture of most high-quality prime lenses. This means you will need more light when using a zoom lens instead of a prime lens, a serious problem when shooting outdoors at night or indoors with artificial lighting. Also, unless you use a very high quality lens, the image quality of a zoom lens will be somewhat inferior to what you would get with a prime lens. A good zoom, however, can be used instead of using several primes, saving you a lot of time during production that would otherwise be spent switching lenses. If the zoom shot is taken with a static camera, an easy technique to maintain sharp focus over the range of the zoom is to first zoom all the way in to your subject and find focus (while the zoom lens is set at its longest focal length). You will then be able to zoom in or out and the subject will remain in focus throughout the shot. If the zoom shot is handheld, you will need a second person to operate the focusing ring, since the camera operator will be busy controlling the zoom ring. A follow focus attachment is indispensable in this case, since it allows a focus puller (the person controlling focus) much easier access to the focusing ring. More expensive solutions include the use of a wireless focusing system, allowing a focus puller to stand a few feet away from the action and still pull focus as needed. Follow focus attachments can also be connected to the zoom ring, letting you control how steadily the zoom is accomplished. An instance where this might be necessary, is when the zoom shot encompasses the entire zoom range of the lens. In this case, you might not be able to turn the focal length ring all the way without having to switch hands at some point, dis-rupting the steadiness of the zoom. Some follow focus attachments can even be adjusted so that a small turn of their knobs results in a longer turn of the zoom ring on the lens, simplifying long zooms (or focusing) tremendously.

format

Most **SD** and **HD** cameras come equipped with a native zoom lens, designed to meet the optical requirements of their electronic components. Unfortunately, the optics inherent in a zoom lens, coupled with the lower sensitivity of the typical **CCD sensor**, make it difficult to shoot in low-light situations without supplementary lighting. When used with a **35mm lens adapter kit**, the light it cuts makes it almost imperative to have extra lights for most situations except when shooting on sunny interiors or exteriors. However, the zoom lenses found on most SD and HD cameras do have an advantage over zooms used in film. With most video cameras, you can change the focal length steadily and smoothly across the entire zoom range with a motorized servo zoom switch. In some prosumer cameras you can even select among various zoom speeds. In film cameras you cannot do this without a motorized follow focus attachment to control the zooming action, as shown in the example from Coppola's *The Conversation*.

lighting

Since zoom lenses tend to be slower than primes, more lights are needed when using them than would be necessary if you were using a prime lens of the same focal length. In these cases, it becomes necessary to weigh the benefits of renting a zoom lens instead of several primes, since any money saved will be offset by the cost of having to rent extra lighting. On the other hand, a zoom can save you a lot of time during production, since you no longer need to switch lenses to change focal length.

breaking the rules

Although this shot appears to have been taken with a zoom lens, it is in fact an optically printed zoom, its magnification created not through zooming during production but with the use of an optical printer in postproduction. The telltale sign of this process is the loss of resolution and increase in graininess as the shot zooms in, an unavoidable side effect since the optical printer is simply rephotographing an already-shot piece of film. In this example, from the opening dream sequence from David Lynch's The Elephant Man (1980), the extra graininess does not feel out of place, adding instead a stylized look to the surreal imagery that visualizes the imagined birth of the titular character.

Kagemusha. *Akira Kurosawa, 1980.*

pan shot

In a pan shot, the camera scans space horizontally pivoting left or right while remaining stationary, mounted on a tripod or even handheld. The term pan is short for panoramic: the showing of an unbroken view of an area. Panning shots are often used to follow a subject as it moves across a location (called pan with shots), and are said to be "motivated" camera moves because the movement of the subject motivates the movement of the camera. Pan shots are also used to shift the view from one subject to another; in these shots, also called pan to shots, the movement of the camera is not motivated by the movement of a subject, making the camera move more apparent to the audience unless some aspect in the narrative internally motivates the pan; for instance, a character looking at something off-screen can motivate a pan that reveals what she is looking at when it traces her gaze. Panning the camera instead of using individual shots to cover a particular aspect of a scene should take into account that a pan preserves the integrity of real time and space, and therefore can convey to an audience that some special connection is taking place that requires its use. For instance, you might want to pan with a character as he moves about a location to establish, in real time, how long it takes him to get across it, or the spatial relationships that exist at that location if this information plays a critical role in your story. Panning can also be used to preserve the integrity of a particularly important performance by an actor that could have its impact diminished if editing were used instead. An argument between a couple, for instance, could be covered by panning back and forth between them instead of using a more typical shot/reverse shot combination, to convey the heightening of emotions as they get increasingly agitated; the panning speed of the camera could even be choreographed to match the intensity of their exchange, while letting the audience experience the argument in real time would make the scene stand out from other scenes that use conventional editing techniques. All of these factors can be considered when trying to decide whether to use a pan shot or a combination of shots to cover a particular scene or moment within a scene in your film.

The example on the left, from Akira Kurosawa's *Kagemusha* (1980), uses a pan with shot to follow the titular character (Tatsuya Nakadai), a lowly thief, as he impersonates a recently deceased general. As he reviews his troops, he gets caught up in the excitement of suddenly being treated as a respected leader, breaking into a furious gallop while his soldiers cheer him. Kurosawa pans with the character as he makes his way by the troops, using a telephoto lens that narrows the field of view considerably. The resulting shot, a Kurosawa stylistic signature, makes the impersonator look like he is moving much faster than he really is because of the telephoto's effect on movement across the x axis of the frame while panning, effectively conveying his unbridled exhilaration in this scene.

This pan shot from Akira Kurosawa's Kagemusha *(1980) takes advantage of the reduced field of view of the telephoto lens to accelerate the perceived motion across the x axis of the frame as it pans with the titular character (Tatsuya Nakadai).*

pan shot

why it works

Panning can be used as an alternative to editing when it is preferable to preserve the integrity of a particularly meaningful performance, relationship, or moment in a scene. In this pivotal scene from Pedro Almodovar's *Broken Embraces* (2009), Mateo (Lluís Homar) enters a bathroom to discover that Lena (Penélope Cruz), his lover and the star of his film was physically abused by her pathologically jealous married lover, a wealthy businessman. The entire scene plays with

out any edits, panning from Lena to Mateo when he enters, then back to Lena when he notices her bloody bruises, culminating in a two shot that maximizes the use of a mirror to show both his reaction and her wounds in the same image. The use of handheld panning within a single shot instead of editing shots of various sizes adds tension and realism to their encounter, letting the audience witness the action as it unfolds in real time.

camera to subject distance used to set the focus was the result of adding the distance from the camera to the mirror, and then from the mirror to the subject (setting the focus exclusively to the surface of the mirror could have resulted in the subject being out of focus).

Placement of the subject's reflection follows the rule of thirds, giving her the proper amount of headroom and resulting in a dynamic composition that complements the dramatic nature of this scene.

A light was placed directly over the sink, highlighting her arm as she washes the blood away. Because this is the brightest area of the frame, the audience's attention will be attracted to it, making this the focal point of the composition.

The inclusion of the subject in the foreground of the frame adds depth the composition and pulls the viewer's gaze toward the focal point of the shot at this stage; the bloody elbow under the faucet.

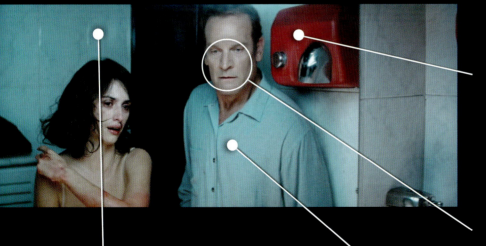

Almodovar's films are known for their thoughtful art direction and creative use of color. In this scene, the bathroom and the man's shirt share the same pale hue of blue, a passive color, perhaps hinting at his inability to help her. The blandness of the bathroom is broken by the vibrant red used on the hand dryer, which also makes the blood on her wounds stand out even more in the composition.

The mirror is cleverly used to let the audience see both the shocked expression on the man's face and her bloody wounds.

The extra headroom over this subject is the result of giving the man the proper amount of headroom for a shot this size. This is an unusual compromise when including two subjects of different heights (although it works within the context of the scene); often, shorter actors are given apple boxes to stand

The composition of the shot was adjusted from an over the shoulder shot to a two shot without cutting, preserving the natural dramatic momentum of the scene and the performance of the actors.

technical considerations

lenses

Since a pan scans space horizontally, your choice of **focal length** can have a major impact in how the audience perceives movement across the **x axis** relative to fixed objects in the foreground and background of the frame. For instance, a pan with shot that follows a subject with a **wide angle lens** will make it look as if he is moving slower across the frame than he is in reality. This effect is the result of the wider **field of view** that shorter focal length lenses have, and becomes more pronounced with wider angle lenses. If the same shot were taken using a **telephoto lens**, the effect would be reversed, with the subject appearing to move faster across the x axis of the frame, as seen in the example from Kurosawa's *Kagemusha* at the beginning of this chapter. Focal length also has an impact on the speed at which you can safely pan without creating a strobing effect, as explained below.

equipment

The panning of the camera should be absolutely steady unless camera shake is part of the visual strategy you designed for your film (by choosing to shoot with a handheld camera, for instance). Any jerkiness will immediately call attention to itself and make the audience aware of the camera, so if a smooth pan is desired, it is imperative to make sure that the tripod head allows you to have precise control over the speed and movement of the panning action. Most tripods come equipped with some resistance mechanism (friction or fluid based) that smooths out panning and tilting to a constant speed; this resistance is adjustable, so that you can pan as slowly or as quickly as necessary with an even pace throughout. Before panning, it is important to make sure the tripod is perfectly level, otherwise the pan will gradually dip or rise; most tripods have a bubble that lets you level the head on which the camera rests precisely for this purpose. It is also important to be aware of the strobing effect that can appear at certain panning speeds when shooting at 24 or 25 fps (with either film or video); if a pan moves beyond a certain speed, strobing, or a stuttering of the image, will be seen. This effect will become more pronounced with longer focal lengths, and will also be affected by the shutter angle being used. The general rule of thumb to prevent strobing is that it should take about 5-7 seconds to pan across the length of the frame; panning at this speed will ensure that the image will not judder (most cinematography manuals have panning speed tables you can consult for this purpose). There is, however, one type of pan in which strobing is of no concern; a swish pan, where the camera snaps from one subject to another, purposely creating a blurry image while in transit. Swish pans are commonly used as transitions between scenes, using the resulting blur to conceal the edit point between two shots. They are sometimes also used within a scene to quickly pan from one subject to another, placing a dramatic emphasis on the subject at the end of the pan.

lighting

Whether you are panning with a subject or panning from one subject to another, the **depth of field** you have will affect your ability to maintain focus throughout the shot. If, for aesthetic or technical reasons, you choose to use a shallow depth of field while panning from a subject to another, you might have to adjust the focus if the second subject if placed at a different distance from the camera than the first subject. However, if you wanted to have all subjects in focus as you pan, you would need to have a deep depth of field, which can only be obtained by using a small aperture that requires enough lighting to avoid underexposing your image. This will of course not be a problem while shooting day exteriors, but might prove challenging while shooting indoors or night exteriors.

breaking the rules

A swish pan (a shot that pans the camera fast enough to create blur) is used in this scene from Edgar Wright's *Hot Fuzz* (2007) to shift the view to top London Cop Nicholas Angel (Simon Pegg) as he arrives to meet his girlfriend Janine (Cate Blanchett), only to find out she has dumped him. Swish pans are commonly used as transitions between scenes, or to place a dramatic emphasis on a subject at the end of the pan when used within a scene. In this example, however, a swish pan is used to conceal an edit within the same scene, and the dramatic emphasis is used as a visual punch line; Wright's work is known for appropriating visual techniques from the horror and science fiction genres for his comedies.

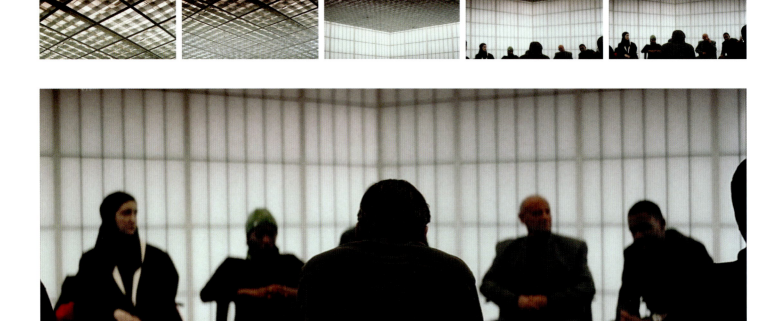

Solaris. *Steven Soderbergh, 2002.*

tilt shot

Tilt shots pivot the camera up or down while it remains stationary, mounted on a tripod or handheld; this move shifts the audience's attention from one area to another, vertically extending the range of the visual scope of the shot. The dynamic frame produced by this vertical move is commonly used as an **establishing shot**, introducing a location by tilting the camera down to gradually reveal it to the audience. Sometimes the tilt ends on a character, showing her arriving or leaving. Another variation includes first showing a character, usually after an exchange with someone, then tilting the camera up to reveal the location, providing a context (i.e., comic or ironic) to their previous exchange. Like **pan shots**, tilt shots preserve the integrity of real time, space, and a performance, so their use should be reserved for those moments in your story when it is narratively meaningful to make this choice rather than using individual shots to cover the same action. The tilting of the camera can be motivated by the movement of a character or some other aspect of the scene (like a character looking up or down at something off-screen that is revealed by a tilt that traces their gaze). Unmotivated camera movement is sometimes avoided because it can call attention to itself and distract the audience from the story; however, there are instances where an unmotivated move can be used to indicate that a special connection exists between two subjects at either end of the tilt shot. For example, tilting from a person standing on the ground to an airplane flying overhead can suggest any number of connections depending on the story's context (i.e. his dream of flying, his desire to return home, the phobia which keeps him from a lover far away, etc.). Tilt shots are substantially less frequently used than pan shots, since most action is commonly staged on the screen along the **x** or **z axes** of the frame; it is rare, for instance, to have an exchange between two characters placed at two substantially different heights that would give you an opportunity to tilt back and forth between them. The most common tilt shots go largely unnoticed by the audience, since they take the form of slight vertical reframes that happen when characters move closer or farther away from the camera, in order to maintain proper **headroom** as per the **rule of thirds**.

A tilt shot is used to establish a connection between a location and a character in this example from Steven Soderbergh's *Solaris* (2002). Part of a brief opening montage that shows a day in the life of troubled psychologist Chris Kelvin (George Clooney), the shot begins with a slow tilt down from the ceiling of a futuristic office to a group therapy session he is conducting. Still reeling from the death of his wife, Chris' life has become stagnant and listless, an expository point that is underlined by the way this tilt shot connects the repetitive pattern of the ceiling and walls, which are also reminiscent of a cage or a cell, to a medium close up that shows him hunched in his chair. This unmotivated camera move is performed slowly enough to effectively create an **abstract shot** when the repeating patterns fill the frame at the beginning of the tilt, while Chris' slow reveal as the camera tilts down makes the visual connection between him and the patterns on the ceiling and the walls hard to miss.

This tilt shot from Steven Soderbergh's Solaris *(2002) creatively connects the repetitive abstract patterns found in this location to convey the predictability and stagnation in Chris Kelvin's (George Clooney) life after the death of his wife.*

tilt shot

why it works

Tilt shots are often used as establishing shots, introducing a location as a character is seen arriving or leaving it. In this example from Martin McDonagh's *In Bruges* (2008), a tilt shot establishes the Belfry tower of Bruges as Ray (Colin Farrell, left) and Ken (Brendan Gleeson, right), Irish hitmen laying low after a botched killing, come to visit it. The shot begins by showing the top of the tower, then quickly tilts down to end in a two-shot of the characters. While the use of a tilt seems merely utilitarian and narratively inconsequential at this stage, it gains tremendous relevance and poignancy as the story progresses, when one the characters seen here jumps to his death from the top of the tower after a climactic scene. Only then is it revealed that the tilting action and the speed of its execution in this shot were foreshadowing that fall - a brilliant example of an image system at work.

tower and the characters at the end of the shot.

its way to the ground.

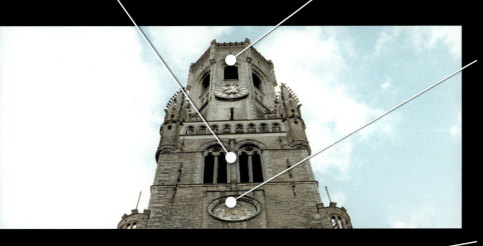

As the camera tilts down to the ground below, real space is preserved, emphasizing the height of the tower. This narrative point could not be conveyed if two shots (one showing the tower and another showing the characters below) had been used instead of the tilt.

The tilt shot ends in a two shot that frames these characters in a medium close up that is also a balanced composition. This shot size allows the audience to focus on the expressions of their faces along with some body language.

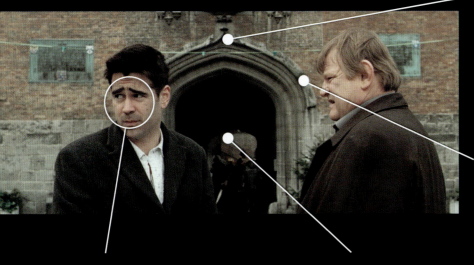

The placement of both subjects roughly follows the rule of thirds (the dot shows the exact location of the top right sweet spot), providing them with the proper amount of headroom for a shot this size, although a bit of a compromise was made since the subject on the right side of the frame is slightly taller than the one on the left. In these cases, the taller subject should be given the correct amount of headroom over the shorter subject.

While a wide angle lens would have distorted the perspective along the z axis at the beginning of the tilt, making the tower seem even taller and the tilt down more pronounced, it would have also distorted the characters at the end of the shot. Instead, a focal length closer to normal was used.

The tilt is doing more than just establishing the location and visually connecting the tower with the characters; the dynamic framing is also foreshadowing an event that will take place later in the story, making the tilting of the camera narratively meaningful.

technical considerations

lenses

The perceived vertical movement of tilt shots, like the horizontal movement of pan shots, can be greatly affected by your choice of **focal length**. **Wide angle lenses** make movement along the **x axis** appear to move slower than in real life (and **telephotos** faster); this also applies to movement along the **y axis** of the frame, although it is less common to have a shot where a character moves upward or downward in the frame that necessitates a tilting move of the camera. A common use of a tilt shot is to establish a location, sometimes also showing a character. In this case, focal length can be chosen according to the dramatic effect the optical distortion produced by a wide angle or telephoto lens can add to the location being established. You might, for instance, choose a wide angle lens for a tilt shot that establishes a building, so that it looks taller and more imposing than in real life. If a telephoto lens were used instead, the building would look much shorter and less imposing.

equipment

Like all dynamic frame shots and camera moves, tilt shots must be executed free of any shakiness unless it is intended (for instance, when a handheld camera is part of your visual strategy). Professional tripod heads come equipped with a fluid or friction based resistance mechanism for this purpose, allowing you to have smooth tilting action at any speed you need. For instance, the fast tilt down in the example from *In Bruges*, on the previous page, would require you to set the friction control to the lowest setting so that the camera pivots quickly yet smoothly. On the other hand, setting the friction control to the highest setting would allow you to create a very slow yet completely smooth tilt like the one used in the example from *Solaris* at the beginning of this chapter. It is also important to make sure that the tripod head is completely level before attempting a tilt, otherwise it will gradually cant towards either side of the frame as you tilt the camera up or down. To prevent this from happening, all you need to do is align the bubble level included on most tripod heads. The speed at which the tilt is executed should take into account the strobing (a juddering of the image) that can occur if the camera is pivoted too quickly, just like in a **pan shot**. Unfortunately, the rule of thumb used to prevent strobing in pan shots cannot be applied to tilt shots, since they move vertically, but it is not that difficult to work out the maximum tilting speed that will not create judder if you account for the **aspect ratio** of the format you are using. For instance, the rule of thumb states that a pan should last from 5-7 seconds to scan the length of a frame to prevent strobing. If your aspect ratio is 1.78:1, a tilt should last 2.8 seconds to scan the height of a frame to avoid strobing. It is also extremely important to make sure the camera's weight is distributed evenly on the tripod head, especially if heavy zooms or big batteries are on board. Most professional tripods come equipped with a sliding base plate mechanism that lets you move the camera backward or forward on the tripod to distribute the weight evenly. An uneven camera can easily tip over during a tilt if its weight is not properly centered on the tripod.

lighting

While tilt shots occur less frequently than pan shots, you might be in a situation where you want to quickly tilt between subjects without having to refocus the lens. In this case, being able to work with a **deep depth of field** will make this possible, provided you have enough light to use a small aperture without underexposing your image. One problem to be aware of is that tilt shots are more prone to catching lens flares from overhead sources of light, making it necessary to reposition them, use French flags to block them from the lens, or move the camera to avoid them, unless they are part of your visual strategy.

breaking the rules

In this beautifully poignant shot, from Wim Wenders' Wings of Desire (1987), a tilt is combined with a dolly in move that gradually tightens the frame to isolate Cassiel (Otto Sander), an angel who comforts lost souls. Uncommonly, in this shot the tilt move takes precedence over the dolly, creating a visually poetic composition that makes the angel appear to rise into the sky.

Ratcatcher. *Lynne Ramsay, 1999.*

dolly shot

Dolly shots are accomplished by placing the camera on a wheeled platform that can be moved smoothly. Although similar to a **zoom shot** (both shots create a dynamic frame with a constantly changing composition along the **z axis**), there are fundamental differences between them. In a zoom shot, the camera remains stationary while the **focal length** of the lens is shifted so the changes in framing are perceived by the audience as if an aspect of the composition is brought closer or moved away from them. Since the dolly shot physically moves the camera while the focal length remains constant, there is a constant change in perspective in the composition, resulting in the audience feeling as if they are the ones moving toward or away from an aspect in the frame. Dolly shots, like all moving camera shots, can be used to reveal, conceal, or comment on an action or situation. An extremely common use of the dolly shot is called the "dolly in," where the camera is brought increasingly closer to the face of a character as he or she makes a meaningful discovery or has to make an important decision. Using a dolly shot instead of cut (to a tighter framing of the face) allows the tension, suspense, and drama of this moment to unfold gradually in real time, while the dynamic composition visually underlines it and makes it stand out from the rest of the scene. Used this way, the dolly shot adds a narrative context that would not be there if only static shots were used, as if commenting on the importance of the moment. Another common use of the dolly shot is the "dolly out" where the camera slowly moves away from a character, usually after an undesirable event has just taken place. The increasingly wider framing in this shot makes the character look gradually smaller in the frame, often indicating a loss of confidence, power, or increasing loneliness or despair. Dolly shots can also be used to reveal an important aspect of a scene that was initially concealed (or vice versa), often accompanying a character who experiences the revelation; the dynamic composition highlights the narrative importance of the discovery, and allows the audience to participate in that experience in real time with the character. Because of the strong visual and narrative statements they can make, dolly shots should be used sparingly, reserved for those moments in the story where the audience should make a strong connection with a situation or a character.

An excellent example of a dolly shot that both reveals an important aspect of a scene and comments on it happens in Lynne Ramsay's *Ratcatcher* (1999), the harrowing tale of a 12 year old boy, James (William Eadie), who comes of age in an impoverished area of Glasgow in the 1970s. After sneaking away on a bus, he arrives at a partially completed housing project set in an idyllic section of the countryside. Inside one of the houses, the camera slowly dollies in to a window as James approaches it, to then follow after him as he jumps out into a wheat field, in one the film's most beautifully surrealistic images. The dolly move gradually reveals the vastness of the field and allows the audience to experience, through the movement of the camera, the exhilaration and magic of this meaningful moment in James' life.

A dolly in visually underlines a surrealistically beautiful moment in the life of James, a 12 year old growing up in an impoverished area of Glasgow, in Lynne Ramsay's Ratcatcher *(1999).*

dolly shot

why it works

One of the most common uses of the dolly shot is as a "dolly in," creating an increasingly tighter framing of a character's face to underline a meaningful moment of discovery or reflection, as seen in this dolly shot from Steven Spielberg's *Raiders of the Lost Ark* (1981). Indiana Jones (Harrison Ford) has just failed to rescue an old flame, Marion (Karen Allen) and believes she is dead. A resourceful man used to facing danger at every turn, he now finds himself unprepared to deal with the real consequences of his adventures. The dolly in tightens the frame from a medium shot that showcases body language and location to a medium close up that concentrates on the pained expression of his face. This camera move cues the audience to the dramatic impact of this emotional moment, and by preserving real time, it also echoes the sudden stop in the narrative flow caused by her death.

The camera to subject distance at this point in the dolly shot resulted in a somewhat deep depth of field, which combined with the wide framing allows the inclusion of much of the activity in the background. As the camera moves closer, the tighter framing and shrinking depth of field separate the character from the surrounding area, letting the audience connect with his pain.

Even though everyone else in the frame is lit with diffused light, the main subject here was lit with the conventional three-point lighting, designed to make him stand out in the composition and to draw the viewers' attention to him. This convention is so widespread that almost no one notices its artifice, even in shots where it should look out of place, like this day exterior shot.

The dolly begins with a medium shot that shows the subject in the center of the frame. This central placement creates a static composition that effectively conveys his current state of mind; he is distraught after the death of his former lover and unable to proceed with his quest.

As the camera approaches the subject, it has to gradually tilt up to adjust the amount of headroom for the new composition of the shot. Compare the cropped head in this framing, proper for a medium close up, to the headroom at the beginning of the dolly shot. The tilt also resulted in a slight low-angle framing, used here against convention (low angles usually suggest power and dominance, not weakness) but necessary because of the camera movement.

The much shorter camera to subject distance has thrown the background out of focus and tightened the frame, showcasing the subject while excluding most of the background. A focus puller made sure that the character remained in focus throughout the length of the shot, a must anytime the camera is moved closer or farther away from a subject.

This bottle peeking into the edge of the frame plays a very important role; it adds depth by adding a layer to what otherwise would be only a two-layer composition (foreground and background), and it suggests the existence of off-screen space, opening the frame.

As the dolly gets closer to frame the subject in a medium close up, a slight change in the composition was carefully executed to give him the proper amount of looking room at the left side of the frame, since that's the direction he is now facing.

technical considerations

lenses

Choosing a lens for a dolly shot will depend on a number of variables, among them: how close to the subject the shot will get, how much of the surrounding are you want the audience to see, how far or close you want the background to appear, and the **depth of field** you need to have at every stage of the shot. While having to consider so many factors might seem daunting at first, it is not as difficult as it appears. A first step is to prioritize the needs of the shot; what is the main narrative point of the dolly move? Is it to showcase the reaction of a character? The way he or she relates to the surrounding area? Both? You might, for instance, pick a lens based on the amount of distortion it will add to the face of a character as the dolly shot ends. Alternatively, you might want the actual movement of the camera toward or away from a character to be underlined visually, choosing a **wide angle lens** to exaggerate the distance covered or a **telephoto** to minimize it. You might also want to include a meaningful aspect of the surrounding area at some point during the beginning or ending of the shot, and therefore choose a **focal length** based on the **field of view** it can give you instead. Depth of field is an important factor if a subject needs to remain in focus over the length of the shot (an exception being a shot where the focus is preset to a given distance, so that only when the camera dollies to that distance the shot comes into focus). If a shallow depth of field is used, it might be extremely hard for the focus puller (the crew member in charge of manipulating the focusing ring on the lens to maintain constant focus on a subject) to do her job, and you might end up choosing a focal length and aperture combination that does not require you to pull focus too often.

equipment

Dolly shots are executed by placing the camera on a moving platform with wheels, which might or might not need tracks. A skateboard dolly, for instance, uses PVC piping for tracks, can be noisy, might need a lot of room (if the dolly shot includes a turn, for instance), and it might take a long time to set up if the terrain is uneven, but it is light and easy to transport. A doorway dolly is a common alternative: it is quiet (critical if you will be recording sound while shooting), does not need tracks, fits through standard size doorways, takes almost no time to set up, and is highly maneuverable. You don't need to restrict yourself to specialized equipment however; any device that will let you move the camera smoothly while keeping an eye on the composition of the shot can be used, like wheelchairs, wheeled tripods, and even homemade solutions. No matter what piece of hardware you use to accomplish the dolly shot, having one will automatically add time to your production schedule, since any shot that includes movement is inherently more difficult to execute and takes extra time to set up, light, and rehearse.

lighting

If the dolly shot is relatively subtle and does not cover much ground, your lighting strategy will not differ much from what you would do if the shot were static. However, if the dolly shot covers a lot of space, for instance going from a long shot to medium close up, things can get complicated, since you then have to light both the location and the character to look visually compelling at every stage of the shot. For instance, if the dolly shot includes a wide field of view and you are using artificial lighting, your sources might have to be placed relatively far from the subject, necessitating much stronger lights than you would need if the dolly shot had a tighter framing. This is why it is important to take into account the lighting needed while considering what lens to use for the dolly (or any other shot).

breaking the rules

Dolly shots are commonly used to underline a meaningful moment in a scene, often when a character makes a discovery or an important decision. This dolly shot from François Ozon's Swimming Pool (2003), the story of a mystery novel writer (Charlotte Rampling) in search of inspiration, does something quite unusual; it moves sideways instead of toward the character, indicating that something unusual is taking place besides her having a sudden burst of creativity. The audience is kept in the dark about the meaning of this shot until the end of the film, where a twist typical of the kind of novels she writes changes the context of everything they have seen.

Taking Lives. D.J. Caruso, 2004.

dolly zoom shot

Also known as a "counter zoom," "contra zoom," "trombone shot," "zolly," and perhaps most famously, the "Vertigo effect" shot, the dolly zoom was introduced to the mainstream cinematic vocabulary in Alfred Hitchcock's *Vertigo* (1958), to visualize the fear of heights experienced by detective John Ferguson (James Stewart) at key moments in the story. The shot is created by using a combination of a **dolly shot** with a **zoom shot**, working in tandem so that as the camera dollies in toward a subject, the lens is zoomed out, or zoomed in if the camera dollies out. The resulting shot, when executed properly, keeps the subject's size constant in the frame while the background perspective changes drastically, appearing to get closer or further away. The effect is extremely overt and unsettling, and is therefore reserved for moments in a story when something especially meaningful is taking place. A very common use of the dolly zoom shot is in situations where a character has a sudden realization, or is surprised by something they see or learn. Other uses include visualizing extreme emotional states, like rage, obsession, falling in love, paranoia, fear, and even drug-induced states. The speed at which the dolly zoom shot is executed can affect the way it is interpreted by the audience and the emotions it can convey. To convey extreme emotions, the dolly zoom is usually performed quickly, making the change in perspective in the background extremely noticeable. In other cases, the dolly zoom is performed very slowly, making the shift in perspective subtle and at times difficult to see; the effect is not as unsettling, conveying that something meaningful, although not necessarily extreme in nature, is taking place. A less common use of the dolly zoom is to showcase the background of the composition instead of a subject in the foreground, who is kept out of focus; in this case the dolly zoom visualizes a character's warped perception of their surroundings, normally due to their state of mind or supernatural influences (a favorite visual trope in Horror films).

The example on the opposite page, from D.J. Caruso's *Taking Lives* (2004), shows the most common use of the dolly zoom shot, as an FBI profiler (Angelina Jolie) helping to catch a serial killer suddenly discovers that a witness she became intimate with is in fact responsible for the murders. The dolly zoom used here starts with the zoom lens set as a **wide angle** and a short camera to subject distance. As the shot progresses, the camera is quickly dollied away while the zoom lens is adjusted into its **telephoto** range, keeping the subject size constant while the background appears to get closer to her (note how much less of the walls in the hallway can be seen in the last frame than in the first frame). The dolly zoom effectively conveys the surprise, disorientation, and shock felt by the character at this critical moment. This shot also demonstrates that when the size of the subject is kept constant, a change in **focal length** does not affect the **depth of field** when counterbalanced by a shift in **camera to subject distance**, as seen in the background, which remains consistently out of focus whether the zoom lens is set to a wide angle (at the beginning of the shot) or a telephoto setting (at the end).

A classic use of the dolly zoom shot is to underline a character's sudden realization that something is wrong, as seen in this example from D.J. Caruso's Taking Lives *(2004).*

dolly zoom shot

why it works

The unusual change in perspective produced by a dolly zoom can visualize a meaningful moment or situation, indicating to the audience that something out of the ordinary is taking place. In this example from Mathieu Kassovitz' *La Haine* (1995), a dolly zoom shot is used to convey how a group of friends raised in the "banlieues" (impoverished French housing projects) feel when they arrive in Paris to collect a debt. Although Vinz (Vincent Cassel, left) and Saïd (Saïd Taghmaoui, right) appear to be indifferent to their surroundings, the dolly zoom reveals how uncomfortable they are when they find themselves outside of their marginalized neighborhood.

As the dolly zoom shot begins, the camera is set close to the subjects, while the zoom lens is set at a short focal length so that it functions as a wide angle. Note the expansion of distances along the z axis of the frame, evidenced by the converging lines of the buildings at a vanishing point at the center of the frame.

The camera is slightly tilted down so that the subjects are shot from a slight high angle, ensuring the inclusion of the buildings in the background. As the camera is dollied away from the subjects, it will have to slightly tilt up to maintain the proper amount of headroom. Note how the top of the handrail is visible in this frame but cannot be seen at the end of the shot (bottom frame), after the camera was tilted up.

The tower in the background is now much larger than it was at the beginning of the shot, but the depth of field has not changed, it has only become more apparent because the long focal length set in the zoom lens has brought it closer to the foreground and enlarged it, making it easier to notice how blurry it was all along. Note the flattening of the perspective in the architectural lines in the background, also caused by the zoom lens now set at a telephoto focal length equivalent.

The size of the characters remains constant, but their facial features are changed since they are first shot with the equivalent of a wide angle lens, which distorts along the z axis, and then with the equivalent of a telephoto lens, which flattens along the z axis. In medium long shots like this one, the change in distortion is not too obvious, but in tighter shots like a medium close up or a close up, they will be more visible.

As the camera was dollied away from the subjects, it was necessary to slightly tilt it up to maintain the proper amount of headroom for a shot this size. Note how the top of the handrail is no longer visible from this angle.

technical considerations

lenses

The zoom ratio of the **zoom lens** you use can determine how drastic the change in perspective in the background will be, and will also affect how much the camera will need to be moved towards or away from subjects to keep them at a constant size in the frame. For instance, the zoom ratio of the lens used in the example on the first page of this chapter, from *Taking Lives*, is not as high as the zoom ratio of the lens used in the example from *La Haine* on the previous page, as seen by the different levels of magnification in their respective backgrounds. A zoom with a high zoom ratio will also make it more challenging to maintain the subjects in focus as the camera is moved, necessitating precise measurements to determine the exact **camera to subject distance** at both ends of the shot. It is also important to determine the amount of distortion that is acceptable to have on the subject, since at both ends of the dolly zoom you will have **wide angle** warping or **telephoto** flattening of facial features. While this might not be too noticeable in a **medium long** or **medium shot**, it might be an issue in **medium close ups** and **close ups**.

equipment

As with a moving camera **zoom shot**, a focus puller will be necessary for a dolly zoom shot, since the camera to subject distance does not remain constant. A follow focus attachment will simplify matters tremendously, especially since the **focal length** ring will also have to be accessed during the shot by the camera operator. The camera can be moved with a dolly, on tracks, with a Steadicam rig, and even handheld, but keep in mind that it will be more difficult to execute the shot properly with a Steadicam or a handheld camera than it will be with a dolly, because of the challenges to choreographing the independent movements of three people (camera operator, focus puller and spotter) instead of hav-

ing them all standing on board a moving dolly. An alternative is to use a wireless system to pull focus remotely while the camera operator manipulates the zoom ring as he or she walks with the camera, but it will still require a lot of practice to do it properly. Regardless of how the camera is moved, it is absolutely essential that the speed at which it moves closer to or away from a subject matches the speed at which the zoom ring is manipulated; otherwise, the subject will seem to grow larger or smaller while the background moves closer or farther away, undoing the effect of a dolly zoom. You will need to do more than a few practice runs to get it right, since you have to coordinate the efforts of the grips moving the dolly, the camera operator manipulating the zoom ring, and the focus puller.

lighting

Since the size of the subject must remain constant in a dolly zoom shot, **depth of field** will mostly be a function of the aperture setting. Camera to subject distance will of course also affect depth of field, but in most instances the dolly zoom shot will not allow you to have the camera sufficiently far away from the subject to throw the background in focus, so its effect in the depth of field will be minimal. The disorienting effect of the dolly zoom can still be produced whether you choose to have a shallow or a deep depth of field (since it is more a function of the zoom ratio of the lens), so your selection can be based on your need to have the background, the foreground, or everything in focus, depending on the needs of your story.

breaking the rules

This shot, from Danny Boyle's Trainspotting (1996), has all the telltale signs of a dolly zoom shot: subject size remains constant, and the background appears to recede into the distance. However, it is not a dolly zoom at all; the bed was simply rolled back along with the camera inside a specially built set. The resulting effect is even more unsettling than in a normal dolly zoom, adding a surreal touch to the depiction of the withdrawal pangs suffered by Renton (Ewan McGregor), a heroin addict on the mend.

The 400 Blows. *François Truffaut, 1959.*

tracking shot

In a tracking shot, the camera is moved to follow the movement of a subject along side it, in front of it (also called a reverse tracking shot, a Kubrick favorite), or behind it; because of this, the movement in tracking shots is said to be motivated. People often confuse tracking shots with **dolly shots**, but they are easy to tell apart, since in dolly shots the camera is moved independently of a subject (an unmotivated type of camera move), dollying towards or away from it, instead of tracking with a moving subject. Tracking shots can be accomplished by placing the camera on a dolly with wheels, or on tracks, with a Steadicam, inside a vehicle, or even handheld, depending on the amount and speed of the subject's movement. Although tracking shots can come in almost any shot size, they are often taken using wider framings, such as **medium shots**, **medium long shots**, and **long shots**, since much of the dynamism of the composition is lost with tighter framings that would exclude most of the surrounding area. Tracking shots that move the camera sideways to follow a subject (a very common setup) have more dynamic compositions than tracking shots where the camera follows from behind or in front of a subject, since they emphasize movement along the **x axis** of the frame. Although less dynamic because they show movement along the **z axis** of the frame, reverse tracking shots have the advantage of letting the audience achieve a higher level of involvement with a character because they show the face of a subject from the front instead of in profile. Sometimes, tracking shots are combined with **zoom shots** or dolly in shots, so that as they follow a character the framing gets increasingly tighter, from a long shot or a medium long shot to a **medium close up** or a **close up**. These combinations can add tension and drama to a meaningful moment in a narrative, underlining the emotions of a character at the end of the shot. Tracking shots are also often long takes, especially when they are used to establish a relationship between a character and the surrounding area; this is often the case with reverse tracking shots, which tend to linger long enough to establish relevant details about a location and a character's reactions as he or she moves through it.

A compelling use of a tracking shot is seen toward the end of François Truffaut's masterpiece *The 400 Blows* (1959), the story of a neglected young Parisian adolescent, Antoine Doinel (Jean-Pierre Léaud), whose mischievous antics put him at odds with his family and eventually land him in a reformatory. Earlier in the film, he expressed his desire to see the ocean, having never seen it before; he soon manages to escape from the institution, only to run aimlessly through the countryside until he catches a glimpse of the coast. His run to freedom is captured in a tracking shot that lasts almost 80 seconds (an eternity in terms of shot length), revealing an emotionless Antoine in a long shot that lets us see the emptiness of his surroundings. The long take preserves the action in real time, dramatizing his escape and the broader impulse for flight (something Antoine does throughout the film), making this a pivotal act within the narrative as it leads the audience to one of the most famous freeze frames in the history of cinema.

A tracking shot stays with Antoine (Jean-Pierre Léaud) for almost 80 seconds as he runs away from a reformatory in François Truffaut's marvelous examination of adolescent psychology, The 400 Blows *(1959).*

tracking shot

why it works

Tracking shots can be combined with other moving camera shots to further emphasize the importance of a moment in a scene. In this example from Tomas Alfredson's *Let the Right One In* (2008), the story of the unlikely friendship that develops between Oskar (Kåre Hedebrant, pictured) a kid who is constantly bullied at school, and Eli (Lina Leandersson), a 200 year old vampire who has remained physically a 12 year old, a tracking shot is combined with a dolly in to underline Oskar's anguish as he is accosted by a classmate. The actor and the camera were blocked so that as the camera tracks alongside him, it also gets closer to him, going from a medium long shot to a medium close up. The bully (Patrik Ridmark) is kept off-screen as Oskar retreats from him, entering the frame only as the tracking shot ends, conveying Oskar's increasing sense of dread and impotence.

The shot remains static until this character enters the frame, motivating the movement of the camera. The framing at this stage of the tracking shot is that of a medium long shot, including the character and much of the surrounding area.

While the camera is still, the audience has a chance to see these two boys play fighting in the background, foreshadowing the threat of violence that pervades this scene and is a central concern of the main character.

The inclusion of this column in the foreground adds depth to the frame and emphasizes the movement of the tracking shot, since it travels across the screen faster than the character in the middle ground.

The headroom in this composition is correct for the bully, but not for his victim in the foreground. Combined with the use of selective focus, this placement ensures the bully is the focal point of the composition. As soon as he leaves, the camera tilts up slightly to give the character in the foreground the right amount of headroom.

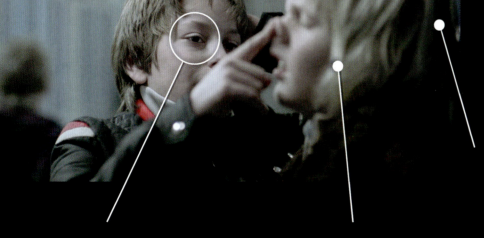

Although this character was placed in the frame according to the rule of thirds, he was not given any room behind him, so that he is shown pressed against the wall and the edge of the frame. This placement underlines the helplessness and inescapability of his situation.

The shallow depth of field allows the use of selective focus, in this case set to the bully in the middle ground instead of the main character in the foreground. This is an unconventional but effective choice that lets the audience identify with the main character by directing their attention to the cause of his distress instead of his facial expressions.

The movement of the camera was set up so that it travels diagonally as it tracks the character, creating an increasingly tighter frame that excludes most of the surrounding area and culminates in a medium close up, visually constricting the character.

technical considerations

lenses

If the tracking shot moves alongside a character, your choice of **focal length** can have a major impact in the way movement across the **x axis** of the frame is perceived. For instance, if a **telephoto lens** is used, the **field of view** will be restricted considerably as the distances along the **z axis** of the frame are compressed. With this setup, even a relatively small sideways move of the camera will appear faster than normal, especially if a tighter framing (like a **medium close up**) is used to cover the action. If a **wide angle lens** is used instead, the field of view will be wider and distances along the z axis extended, making the background look farther away than it is in reality. Movement across the x axis will also appear to be slower than normal, since the background will not pass across the frame as quickly as when using a telephoto lens. When performing a handheld tracking shot, wide angle lenses and short **camera to subject distances** are commonly used, since they hide camera shake considerably. Remember, telephoto lenses will exaggerate any camera movement, and are usually recommended only when the camera is moved using a dolly, on tracks, with a vehicle, or with some stabilizing device like a Steadicam. Focusing can be problematic in a tracking shot, especially if a moving subject angles away from the camera, or when the shot combines sideways movement with a dolly in or out move, as seen in the example from *Let the Right One In* on the previous page. Since the camera to subject distance will not remain constant in these cases, a focus puller will have to assist to maintain sharp focus throughout the shot, after key distances have been measured and the shot choreographed and rehearsed a few times.

equipment

Using wheeled dollies can save a lot of time in the setup of tracking shots provided the surface over which they need to travel is even and smooth; otherwise, using a dolly that moves over tracks is an option, but keep in mind that it might take a long time to set the tracks up, especially if the terrain is very uneven. Other alternatives are to hand hold the camera, or use a Steadicam system or some other device for stabilization. It is important to remember that whenever the camera is handheld, the distance between it and the subject is likely to change throughout the shot, making it essential to find a way to adjust focus during a shot. This can be accomplished with a wireless focus pulling system, a camera assistant/focus puller using a follow focus attachment (although this is easier said than done), or by the camera operator herself, focusing not by manipulating the focusing ring on the lens, but by maintaining a constant camera to subject distance with the help of a large preview monitor attached to their camera rig. Another option to maintain sharp focus is to set up the tracking shot so that there is a relatively long distance between the camera and the subject (as seen in the example on the opposite page, from Florian Henckel von Donnersmarck's 2006 film, *The Lives of Others*), but doing this will necessarily affect the composition of your shot.

lighting

Lighting can also be manipulated to make it easier to keep your subject in focus; for instance, you could add enough lights so that you can use a smaller aperture on the lens that gives you a deeper **depth of field**, allowing more room for the camera operator to move without throwing the subject out of focus. When shooting outdoors during the day, having enough light will not be a problem, unless a shallow depth of field is desired, which will require the use of a larger aperture on the lens. For this reason, any shooting done during the day outdoors should always include **ND filtration**, to control how much light will reach your film. Some **SD** and **HD** video cameras come equipped with ND filtration switches precisely for this purpose.

breaking the rules

Tracking shots are motivated by the movement of characters in the frame, a convention designed to avoid camera movement that calls attention to itself. In this tracking shot from Florian Henckel von Donnersmarck's The Lives of Others (2006), the camera follows Hauptmann Wiesler (Ulrich Mühe), a former Stasi (East Germany's secret police) officer, some years after the fall of the Berlin wall. At one point during the tracking shot the camera stops, allowing him to leave the frame for a couple of seconds. This seemingly unmotivated action by the camera is jarring and unexpected, creating a moment of tension that lasts until the character steps back into the frame, as if suddenly realizing something; the shot ends as he stands in front of a large poster advertising a book by a counterrevolutionary playwright he spied on yet chose to protect rather than arrest.

Goodfellas. *Martin Scorsese, 1990.*

Steadicam shot

While dollies on wheels and tracks can effectively create smooth and expressive camera movement, their implementation can be difficult and limiting at times; for instance, no dollies or tracks can be used to move a camera up or down a set of stairs. Garret Brown's invention of the Steadicam in 1976 solved this problem, adding a new kind of shot to the cinematic vocabulary available to filmmakers: the Steadicam shot. A Steadicam rig involves the use of a special vest with an articulated arm to which a camera is attached and stabilized with a gimbal system; the rig effectively isolates any shakiness caused by the movement of the operator, allowing for almost unlimited freedom of movement (restricted solely by the endurance of the person wearing the rig). Steadicam shots that use an actual Steadicam rig or a similar stabilizing camera mount (from companies like MK-V, Chrosziel, Glidecam, and Manfrotto, among others) can replicate the moves of **dolly shots** and **tracking shots**, with the added benefit of being able to also boom the camera up and down or do a 360° shot around a character and any other move in between. Steadicam shots are commonly reserved for times when maintaining the integrity of time, space, and the fluidity of movement are narratively meaningful to the story; there should be a compelling reason why a particular scene is covered, for instance, with a Steadicam shot instead of using a combination of shots of various sizes. Sometimes, a Steadicam shot will be used to preserve the unity of a performance by a character or characters in a single take, reframing the composition of the shot as needed to increase the involvement of the audience or to underline a particular aspect of the scene. The preservation of real time heightens the tension and generates the anticipation that anything can happen, since there are no edits to signal to the audience something particularly meaningful is taking place. In some cases, the fluidity and smoothness of the camera movement is integral to the narrative point of the shot, commenting on the action that is being presented. The freedom of movement that these shots allow are also used to give the viewer a feeling that they are there, amongst the action and activity in the scene. Like most moving camera shots, Steadicam shots tend to be motivated by the movement of a character, and are therefore meant to feel organic to the flow of a scene.

A brilliant example of a Steadicam shot can be seen in Martin Scorsese's *Goodfellas* (1990), when Henry Hill (Ray Liotta), an up and coming gangster, takes his girlfriend Karen (Lorraine Bracco) out for dinner. In a virtuosic Steadicam shot, we follow them as they enter a popular restaurant through a side door, bypassing a large crowd waiting in line to get in. After a labyrinthine walk through hallways and a hectic kitchen, they make their way into the main seating area, bypassing another line of patrons waiting impatiently to be seated. Finally, they are promptly given a table right next to the stage, as Henry tips everyone from bouncers to waiters. The use of a single Steadicam shot to cover this sequence (instead of using a series of shots or various sizes) allows the audience to tag along with the couple, letting them experience the privilege and status that comes with living life as a "goodfella."

The fluidity and smoothness of this Steadicam shot is used to let the audience experience what it is like to enjoy the special perks of being a "goodfella" in Martin Scorsese's Goodfellas *(1990).*

Steadicam shot

why it works

The Steadicam shot can be used to maintain the unity of an actor's performance in real time while also reframing to create dramatic emphasis, heightening tension and allowing the audience to connect with a scene. In this riveting example from Tony Gilroy's *Michael Clayton* (2007), a single Steadicam shot is used to maximum effect, becoming at times a two shot, a medium close up, an O.T.S. shot, a long shot, a close up, and finally a medium shot, as we follow two ter-

rifyingly efficient killers for hire (Terry Serpico and Robert Prescott) while they murder a litigator for a chemical company who decided to sabotage the case against them (Tom Wilkinson). The use of a single Steadicam shot, instead of a series of shots edited together for dramatic effect, highlights the killers' swift efficiency and suggests they have done this many times before.

A tight framing was used at the beginning of the shot to exclude a lot of off-screen space, allowing one killer to enter the frame suddenly, even though he was only a couple of feet away. From this moment forward, the Steadicam operator will reframe the composition to let the audience see relevant details and to add dramatic emphasis to the scene.

The various compositions needed from this Steadicam shot made it imperative to carefully choreograph the action beforehand, so that focus could be maintained on the various subjects. At this stage of the shot, for instance, the camera was focused on the subjects in the foreground, evidenced by the blurry background.

Keeping proper headroom in a moving shot can be challenging, especially when the action includes sudden movements. Steadicam operators need to be experts at constantly predicting subject movement and assessing the composition of the frame, in addition to carrying the rig and using their peripheral vision to move safely through a location.

Although upside down, the subject was placed in the frame according to the rule of thirds, in this case over the bottom left sweet spot; the diagonal placement of the body across the frame reinforces this placement by leading the viewer's gaze toward his face, the focal point of this composition.

As the camera reframed the subject for this composition, focus had to be adjusted to make sure his face would be sharp. Compare this shallower depth of field with the deep depth of field in the fourth frame on the opposite page, when the Steadicam shot was reframed into a long shot.

technical considerations

lenses

Unlike a handheld shot, a stabilizing rig does not necessitate the use of a **wide angle lens** to hide camera shake. Your **focal length** choice can be dictated by your need to have a particular **field of view**, or to make the background appear closer or farther away from a subject, or to manipulate the perception of movement as the camera travels. In a static composition, it is relatively easy to gauge what focal length will best fit your needs; the dynamic frame of a moving shot, however, will present you with many compositional possibilities depending on the lens you pick. For instance, if the Steadicam shot will include a lot of movement along the **z axis**, you might want to exaggerate the distance covered by the camera by using a **wide angle lens**, making objects or characters coming toward or away from the lens appear to swish by. Alternatively, you might want to make it look as if a character is hardly moving along the z axis at all, and use a **telephoto lens** that compresses these distances instead. These spatial distortions can also produce a very distinctive effect when using the camera at a low or high angle, as seen in Stanley Kubrick's *The Shining* (1980), where a wide angle lens was used to make the walls of a hedge maze appear much taller than they actually were. Another important consideration when choosing a lens for a Steadicam shot is the minimum focusing distance you need to have between camera and subject. For instance, you might want to maintain a constant composition that includes the camera following very close behind or in front of a moving subject, necessitating the use of a shorter focal length lens that will allow a very close camera to subject distance (also making it possible to blur the background). Conversely, a longer focal length will have a longer minimum focusing distance, forcing you to keep the camera farther back from the subject (making it more difficult to blur the background).

equipment

While the Steadicam has become synonymous with the use of stabilized shots, there are a number of solutions available for virtually every format of film and video cameras. However, only higher-end solutions will give you more options to set up the camera (for instance, to place the camera close to the ground, or provide you with enough support to let you operate heavier cameras for longer periods of time). The use of large preview monitors to let operators gauge the composition and focus of the shot at a glance is imperative, since they will also have to use their peripheral vision or a spotter (an assistant that guides the operator, especially when walking backwards) to safely walk or even run while shooting; the flip-out LCD screens found in most **SD** and **HD** video cameras are simply not large enough for this purpose.

lighting

Dynamic camera shots always present a challenge for the Director of Photography, because a moving camera will make it extremely difficult or even impossible to hide movie lights in a location. One strategy is to carefully choreograph the path of the camera to avoid showing lights, but doing this will add another level of difficulty to an already demanding shot. Another strategy is to light the entire location with practicals (lights that are part of the mise en scène) relamped with higher-wattage bulbs. The movement of actors is then blocked so that they will be lit by these lights, allowing the camera to move more freely. Lighting also plays a critical role in controlling **depth of field**; this is especially important in a Steadicam shot because focus is often accomplished by the operator maintaining a constant **camera to subject distance**. If the depth of field is too shallow, it is more difficult to keep the subject consistently within the area of sharp focus, which might be exactly what you want as part of a visual strategy you could design for your film.

breaking the rules

The movement of Steadicam shots is often motivated by the movement of a subject, since unmotivated camera movement can be confused as being a subjective shot from an unseen observer. Several key Steadicam shots in Stanley Kubrick's Full Metal Jacket (1987) blur this distinction, by placing the camera low to the ground and behind Marines as they enter dangerous areas in this film about the dehumanizing effects of war; these shots effectively place audiences in the middle of the action, as if they were Marines themselves.

Crouching Tiger, Hidden Dragon. *Ang Lee, 2000.*

crane shot

In a crane shot, the camera is mounted on a support that can be an actual crane, a jib arm, a cherry picker, or any other device that will allow the camera to be moved vertically, horizontally, or in a combination of both. The typical crane shot, however, emphasizes a vertical move of the camera that can encompass anywhere from just a few feet all the way up to more than one hundred feet in height. Although there are many variations, crane shots are most commonly used to gradually reveal the grand scale of a location or environment as the camera is moved upward, including more details as the camera's vantage point gets higher. This type of crane shot can work essentially as an **establishing shot**, edited at the beginning of a scene or whenever a key location is introduced. The same crane move is also often used to gradually change the framing from a tight shot of a character to a wide shot of a location as the character recedes into the distance, usually at the end of a key scene or even the end of a film. Another extremely common crane shot essentially reverses this move, starting with a long or even an extreme long shot that includes a large area of a location that then moves downward into a tighter framing of a character, isolating her in the composition. The upward or downward movement of the camera in a crane shot can be made more apparent if there are objects in the foreground of the composition that pass by it as it is moved. These foreground elements might not be necessary if the crane shot elevates the camera significantly, since the change in vantage point will be very apparent in those cases; however, if the crane shot elevates the camera only a few feet and the subject is relatively distant from it, the move might go completely unnoticed unless something passes by the camera in the foreground of the composition. Crane shots can also be combined with other types of cam-era movement, by incorporating the use of dollies or other types of moving platforms that can add a great level of complexity to a shot (most notably in **sequence shots**). The use of a crane shot to introduce a location, a character, or to underline a key event, will make a powerful narrative statement that can convey there is something especially meaningful or relevant taking place, since the shift in the composition is accompanied by a shift in our understanding of the narrative meaning of the shot; its use should therefore be reserved only for those moments in your story where you want that shift in the minds of the audience to take place.

A classic use of a crane shot occurs in Ang Lee's *Crouching Tiger, Hidden Dragon* (2000), during an extended flashback sequence where Jiao Long Yu (Zhang Zi-Yi), a member of an aristocratic family with a secret passion for martial arts, meets Lo "Dark Cloud" (Cheng Chang), the leader of a gang of desert bandits who ends up falling for her. Lo is introduced with a crane shot that gradually reveals him and his gang, combined with a tilting move of the camera that dramatically changes the vantage point from a low angle to a high angle. The visual emphasis conveyed by the use of a crane shot to introduce this character clearly suggests his importance in the story, and the fact that this territory is his domain. This use is a common technique designed to make a vivid first impression in the minds of the audience.

Ang Lee's Crouching Tiger, Hidden Dragon *(2000) uses a crane shot to dramatically reveal a gang of desert bandits and their leader, Lo (Cheng Chang).*

crane shot

why it works

In addition to introducing narratively important locations or characters, crane shots can, like other dynamic camera moves, also underline especially poignant moments. In Jane Campion's *The Piano* (1993), a crane shot is used when Ada (Holly Hunter), a mute Scottish woman who moves to New Zealand as part of an arranged marriage, decides to obey her husband and give piano lessons to the man who has her beloved piano so she can get it back. The dramatic emphasis conveyed by a descending crane shot externalizes the emotional turmoil caused by her decision to act against her will.

The camera is tilted down at the beginning of the crane shot, producing a high angle, nearly over-head view of the subjects and the immediate area. As the crane shot continues, the camera will be tilted up and panned slightly to frame the main subject into a medium close up from a more neu-tral angle. The combination of a crane shot, with a tilt, and a pan makes this rather small camera move more dramatic than if it were just a crane shot.

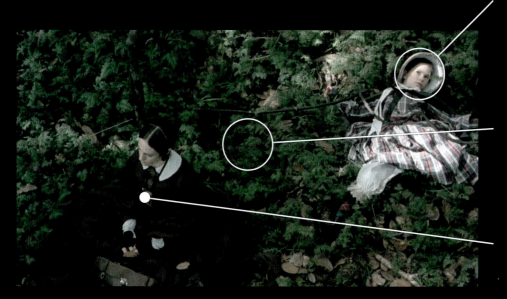

The camera to subject distance and aperture com-bination produced a depth of field that kept both subjects and the surrounding area in sharp focus. As the crane shot lowers the camera, the distance to the main subject becomes shorter, creating a shallow depth of field that centers the audience's attention on her.

The placement of subjects at the beginning of the crane shot does not follow the rule of thirds, using an unorthodox framing instead that emphasizes the visual conflict between Victorian manners and the exuberance of the New Zealand jungle.

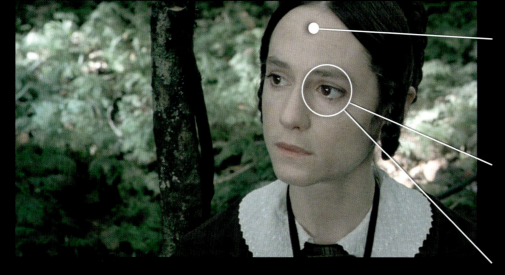

At the end of the crane shot, the camera was tilted up into a less severe high angle and slightly panned to frame this subject into a conventional medium close up that follows the rule of thirds, giving her the proper headroom and looking room for a shot this size.

The much shorter camera to subject distance re-quired the lens to be refocused to the main sub-ject. When using a crane, this is commonly accom-plished with the use of remote heads that allow an operator to manipulate the focus, panning, tilting, and zooming from a distance.

Note the use of an eyelight to avoid giving her eyes a "dead gaze," as well as the diffused light over her face to soften the shadows in this otherwise sunny

technical considerations

lenses

Your choice of **focal length** will of course depend on the type of crane shot, the blocking of the subjects within the composition, and the narrative point you are trying to make. For instance, a crane shot that gradually expands the frame as it elevates the camera to include a large area of a location (a common use of a crane shot to end a scene) would benefit from the use of a **wide angle lens**, since its wide **field of view** would let you include more of the location than if you used a **telephoto lens**. Conversely, a crane shot that emphasizes the upward movement of the camera by including elements in the foreground will appear to move faster when using a telephoto lens instead of a wide angle lens, because of the way they tend to distort movement along the **x and y axes** of the frame. Other variables that should influence your choice of focal length could include the amount of distortion you might want to add or exclude at some point in the crane shot. For instance, in the example from Campion's *The Piano* on the previous page, the crane shot ends with a **medium close up** of a subject that would look significantly different if a wide angle or a telephoto lens had been used, since they would have distorted her features. Since crane shots can encompass a complex set of camera and subject movement, keep in mind that your choice of focal length can potentially work against the point of your shot if you ignore how it affects field of view and movement across all axes of the frame.

equipment

As with all dynamic camera moves, even the simplest crane shot will require extra time to set up, choreograph, and shoot; you should always account for this when planning your production schedule. There are over a hundred different models of cranes available for film and video production, anywhere from a jib arm that attaches to a tripod letting you elevate and lower the camera just a few feet, to large 8000 pound cranes that require at least two operators, and let you raise the camera over 100 feet. Other options include telescopic cranes, cranes with articulated arms, cranes that can suspend a Steadicam operator, motorized cranes that can cruise at highway speeds, and cranes that can support the weight of a large camera and two operators on a platform. One thing to keep in mind is that unless the crane can support an operator in addition to the camera, you will need some way to preview the frame as the crane shot is executed. This is accomplished with the use of a preview monitor attached at the end of the arm, letting the operator see the framing of the shot. However, this setup will not allow you to control focusing, zooming, panning, or tilting, unless the crane comes equipped with a motorized remote head to access these features. It is also extremely important to always remember that regardless of the crane type you are using, you must take extra safety precautions on the set (like never allowing anyone to walk under a crane, only letting qualified personnel operate it, never exceeding its weight and movement restrictions, making cast and crew aware of the movement that will be executed, and being aware of overhead power lines in the immediate area).

lighting

If the crane shot is taken outdoors during the day and a character is an integral part of the shot, lighting considerations will involve finding a way to diffuse the sunlight over her in a way that does not interfere with the rising or lowering movement of the camera, which might be difficult to do depending on the angle of incidence of the light. Crane shots taken on night exteriors can also present you with same problems you will encounter when taking long or extreme long shots under the same conditions; you will have to use powerful lights positioned at a high vantage point that can cover a wide area, or find a location with enough available light for this purpose.

breaking the rules

Crane shots are often combined with other camera moves (like pans and tilts) to augment the dramatic impact of a meaningful moment in a narrative. This example from Sergio Leone's Once Upon a Time in the West (1968) adds even more complexity by also seamlessly incorporating a zoom out, a dolly out, and a tilt of the camera to a crane shot as it pulls back to reveal the sadistic killing of a man. Throughout the film, we followed "Harmonica" (Charles Bronson) as he relentlessly tracked down Frank (Henry Fonda), the leader of gang of ruthless killers, without knowing his motives. During their final showdown, Frank (and the audience) finally learns that years ago he had viciously killed Harmonica's brother, during a flashback that uses a complex crane shot to convey the momentous significance of this event.

Touch of Evil. *Orson Welles, 1958.*

sequence shot

Sequence shots are among the most complex, difficult, and ultimately rewarding shots you can attempt. The term comes originally from the literal translation of the French "plan-séquence," and refers to a shot that incorporates a sophisticated set of dynamic camera moves and framing over a long take, very often encompassing action from several scenes that would otherwise be covered with a number of separate shots. Sequence shots make an unmistakably powerful narrative statement about the importance of the action they cover and the spatial and temporal relationships between elements in the shot, and therefore they are often used to showcase a crucial set of events that are pivotal to the understanding of the rest of the film. Sequence shots can include **crane shots**, **dolly shots**, **zoom shots**, handheld shots, panning, tilting, **tracking shots**, and **Steadicam shots**, often combined seamlessly to create a dynamic frame that can go anywhere from an **extreme close up** to an **extreme long shot**. Camera movement in sequence shots is often motivated by the movement of characters, although unmotivated camera movement is also used, exclusively or in combination with motivated movement. Since sequence shots always use long takes (shots that can last anywhere from a minute to well over an hour, depending on the shooting format), they preserve real time, space, and the performance of actors, and can add realism, tension, and dramatic emphasis to a scene. However, this real time aspect does not automatically connote realism, as these shots are frequently stylistically virtuosic and very apparent to audiences. Because of the complexity of sequence shots, filmmakers have found ways to cheat, creating what appear to be extended sequence shots that are in fact a number of separate, mini-sequence shots with their edits concealed. This is often accomplished by cutting between two shots while the frame is completely filled with a nondescript image, like an blank wall or the shadow of a character as she passes in front of the camera, a technique used most famously in Alfred Hitchcock's film *Rope* (1948). More recently, the advent of computer generated imagery, or CGI, has made it possible to conceal edits more effectively, making them virtually impossible to detect.

One of the most famous examples of a sequence shot happens during the opening scene in Orson Welles' *Touch of Evil* (1958). The shot begins with a close up of a homemade explosive, which is placed in the trunk of a car that later gets driven by a couple on their way to the United States-Mexico border. Their car crosses paths with a newlywed couple (Charlton Heston and Janet Leigh) also on their way to the border, whose romantic interlude is interrupted by the explosion of the car. This entire set of events is astoundingly and flawlessly covered with a single three-minute sequence shot (accomplished with the use of a camera mounted on a crane in the back of a truck) that lets the action unfold in real time, amplifying the suspense and tension set up at the beginning of the shot when the explosive's timer was set. The intricate camera movement also introduces the border area in a way that is suggestive of the tangled moral, ethical, legal, and cultural clashes that will occur there afterward, one of the key themes explored in this film.

This legendary sequence shot from the opening scene of Orson Welles' Touch of Evil (1958) allows the action to unfold in real time, gradually intensifying the suspense and tension initially introduced when an explosive device on a timer is shown being triggered at the beginning of the shot.

sequence shot

why it works

Sequence shots can make a powerful narrative statement that showcases a pivotal and extended set of events, preserving the integrity of time, space, and performance in the process. This crucial scene from Juan José Campanella's *The Secret in Their Eyes* (2009) does just that, in an amazing sequence shot (actually seven shots seamlessly merged with the aid of CGI) that begins high above a soccer stadium,

glides above the crowds and follows federal justice agents Benjamin and Pablo (Ricardo Darín and Guillermo Francella) as they chase after a murder suspect (Javier Godino, pictured) through the bowels of the stadium, ending with his arrest on the playing field. The extreme dramatic emphasis conveyed by the sequence shot underlines the importance his capture represents and all but confirms his guilt.

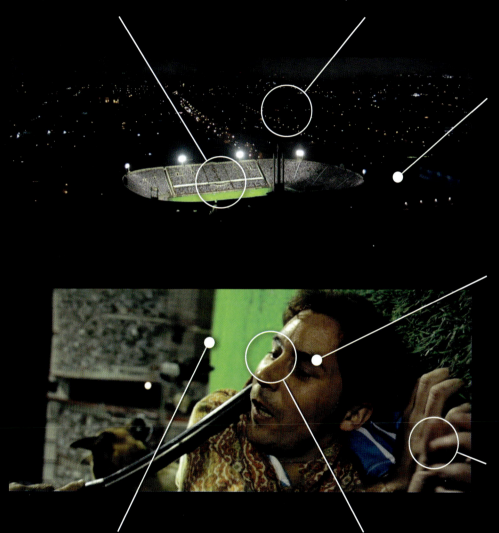

The sequence shot begins with a helicopter shot that reveals a soccer stadium while a match is in progress. This dramatic reveal is narratively justified by the agents' previous discovery that their suspect is a passionate soccer fan and would never miss a game of his favorite team.

This section of the sequence shot would lose much of its visual impact if the stadium were surrounded by brightly lit buildings. Instead, the darkness around the stadium makes its brightly lit interior stand out in the composition.

The sequence shot uses a dynamic framing that shifts the composition from an extreme long shot, taken from hundreds of feet into the air, to a medium close up only a few inches from the ground. This seemingly impossible feat was accomplished by seamlessly blending seven separate shots with the aid of CGI.

Subject placement follows the rule of thirds, placing him over the top right sweet spot of the frame. This ensures a dynamic composition with the proper amount of headroom and looking room, even in this extremely canted shot.

The camera to subject distance and large aperture combination used in this shot resulted in a shallow depth of field that effectively isolates him in the composition, reflecting his stressful emotional state as he is being arrested.

The use of an extremely canted camera (almost a full 90 degrees) at the end of the sequence shot is suggestive of this character's abnormal psychology, even though only the background is off kilter.

Although this subject is supposed to be lit only by the stadium's available light, his lighting was tweaked so that it matches the dramatic tone of this scene, using light sources of different intensities instead of the flat, even lighting of a professional sports arena.

technical considerations

lenses

The complexity of the sequence shot will dictate the appropriate **focal length(s)** or even the kind of lens that will work best for the job. Some factors to consider are: the variety of shot sizes you will be attempting, the **field of view** necessary at every stage of the shot, the type of camera or subject movement that needs to be emphasized or understated, the minimum **camera to subject distance** the shot requires, whether a zoom lens will be needed to expand the dynamic frame choices, the need to have a specific maximum aperture, and many other variables. In Welles' *Touch of Evil*, the use of a relatively **wide angle lens** elongated distances and exaggerated movement along the **z axis** of the frame, added some optical distortion to the architecture of the border town, and produced a wide field of view that allowed the inclusion of much of the richly detailed mise en scène. These qualities reflect the importance the border town plays in the story and present it as a labyrinthine, sleazy, and sinister place, filled with moral and ethical ambiguities. While this example represents a perfect incorporation of visual style and theme, the technical requirements of a sequence shot will sometimes override your desire to use a particular focal length. The same sequence shot, for instance, would have been nearly impossible to shoot with a telephoto lens and a shallow **depth of field**.

equipment

Sequence shots can require virtually any kind of equipment designed to create a free-flowing dynamic camera move, including cranes, jibs, dollies, vehicles, helicopters, Steadicam rigs, and even a handheld camera. While all dynamic camera moves require extra time to light and to coordinate equipment, crew, resources, and cast, the unique technical requirements of a sequence shot simply cannot be overstated. In fact, it is entirely possible for a sequence shot to take up an entire day of shooting or more, depending on the level of complexity it entails; for instance, it took Michelangelo Antonioni 11 days to shoot a 7-minute sequence shot for his film *The Passenger* (1975).

lighting

The strategies for lighting a sequence shot are not too dissimilar from the ones used for **Steadicam shots** and other dynamic camera moves that cover a single wide area or numerous distinct spaces. If shooting night interiors, the use of practicals (sources of light visible within the frame that are part of the mise en scène) can be extremely helpful, since a roaming camera is likely to prevent you from placing movie lights where you normally would. In some cases, a crew member is enlisted to travel alongside the camera with a portable light source to provide sufficient and constant exposure to a moving subject, although this raises the level of complexity of an already technically demanding shot. Day interiors can be lit using only motivated light coming through windows, allowing the camera to travel freely without worrying about the placement of lights within the location. Night exteriors, as always, present a formidable challenge unless you have access to large lighting fixtures that can be raised high enough to pass for moonlight, even though it would never be that bright in real life. Another option would be finding a location with enough available light so that very few additional lights, if any, would be needed (as seen in the sequence shot example from Campanella's *The Secret in Their Eyes*). More often than not, it will be extremely hard or even impossible to have perfect lighting throughout an entire sequence shot, so you should decide beforehand what the key moments are so that you can choreograph and light them accordingly.

breaking the rules

It is impossible to overstate the spectacular achievement accomplished in Aleksandr Sokurov's Russian Ark (2006), a film that uses a single, 91-minute Steadicam sequence shot to transport the audience through 300 years of Russian history as they explore the Hermitage Museum. This shot incorporates virtually every type of shot described in this book, and it was made possible thanks to the use of a Steadicam and a portable hard drive recording system.

filmography

3 Monkeys. Dir. Nuri Bilge Ceylan. Zeyno Film, 2008.

The 400 Blows. Dir. François Truffaut. Les Films du Carrosse, 1959.

Amélie. Dir. Jean-Pierre Jeunet. Claudie Ossard Productions, 2001.

Apocalypto. Dir. Mel Gibson. Icon Entertainment International, 2006.

The Baader Meinhof Complex. Dir. Uli Edel. Constantin Film Produktion, 2008.

Bad Boy Bubby. Dir. Rolf de Heer. Australian Film Finance Corporation, 1993.

Barry Lyndon. Dir. Stanley Kubrick. Peregrine, 1975.

Being John Malkovich. Dir. Spike Jonze. Gramercy Pictures, 1999.

Being There. Dir. Hal Ashby. Lorimar Film Entertainment, 1979.

The Blair Witch Project. Dirs. Daniel Myrick and Eduardo Sánchez. Haxan Films, 1999.

Blue Velvet. Dir. David Lynch. De Laurentiis Entertainment Group, 1986.

The Bourne Supremacy. Dir. Paul Greengrass. Universal Pictures, 2004.

Brazil. Dir. Terry Gilliam. Embassy International Pictures, 1985.

Broken Embraces. Dir. Pedro Almodóvar. Universal Pictures International, 2009.

Children of Men. Dir. Alfonso Cuarón. Universal Pictures, 2006.

City of God. Dirs. Fernando Meirelles and Kátia Lund. O2 Filmes, 2002.

Clockers. Dir. Spike Lee. 40 Acres & A Mule Filmworks, 1995.

The Conversation. Dir. Francis Ford Coppola. American Zoetrope, 1974.

Crouching Tiger, Hidden Dragon. Dir. Ang Lee. Columbia Pictures Film Production Asia, 2000.

Die Hard. Dir. John McTiernan. Twentieth Century Fox Film Corporation, 1988.

The Diving Bell and the Butterfly. Dir. Julian Schnabel. Pathé Renn Productions, 2007.

Dogville. Dir. Lars von Trier. Zentropa Entertainments, 2003.

The Elephant Man. Dir. David Lynch. Brooksfilms, 1980.

Exiled. Dir. Johnnie To. Media Asia Films, 2006.

Fallen Angels. Dir. Kar Wai Wong. Jet Tone Production, 1995.

Full Metal Jacket. Dir. Stanley Kubrick. Warner Bros. Pictures, 1987.

Gattaca. Dir. Andrew Niccol. Columbia Pictures Corporation, 1997.

The Godfather. Dir. Francis Ford Coppola. Paramount Pictures, 1972.

Gomorrah. Dir. Matteo Garrone. Fandango, 2008.

Goodfellas. Dir. Martin Scorsese. Warner Bros. Pictures, 1990.

The Graduate. Dir. Mike Nichols. Embassy Pictures Corporation, 1967.

Hero. Dir. Yimou Zhang. Elite Group Enterprises, 2002.

Hidden. Dir. Michael Haneke. Les Films du Losange, 2005.

Hot Fuzz. Dir. Edgar Wright. Working Title Films, 2007.

I am Legend. Dir. Francis Lawrence. Warner Bros. Pictures, 2007.

In Bruges. Dir. Martin McDonagh. Focus Features, 2008.

Inglourious Basterds. Dir. Quentin Tarantino. Universal Pictures, 2009.

Into the Wild. Dir. Sean Penn. Paramount Vantage, 2007.

Jeanne Dielman, 23 Quai du Commerce, 1080 Bruxelles. Dir. Chantal Akerman. Paradise Films, 1975.

Kagemusha. Dir. Akira Kurosawa. Toho Company, 1980.

La Haine. Dir. Mathieu Kassovitz. Canal+, 1995.

Last Year at Marienbad. Dir. Alain Resnais. Cocinor, 1961.

Leon: The Professional. Dir. Luc Besson. Gaumont, 1994.

Let the Right One In. Dir. Tomas Alfredson. EFTI, 2008.

The Lives of Others. Dir. Florian Henckel von Donnersmarck. Wiedemann & Berg Filmproduktion, 2006.

The Marriage of Maria Braun. Dir. Rainer Werner Fassbinder. Albatros Filmproduktion, 1979.

The Matrix Reloaded. Andy Wachowski and Lana Wachowski. Warner Bros. Pictures, 2003.

Memories of Murder. Dir. Joon-ho Bong. CJ Entertainment, 2003.

Michael Clayton. Dir. Tony Gilroy. Samuels Media, 2007.

Misery. Dir. Rob Reiner. Castle Rock Entertainment, 1990.

Mystery Train. Dir. Jim Jarmusch. JVC Entertainment Networks, 1989.

Naked. Dir. Mike Leigh. Thin Man Films, 1993.

Nineteen Eighty-Four. Dir. Michael Radford. Umbrella-Rosenblum Films Production, 1984.

Oldboy. Dir. Chan-wook Park. Show East, 2003.

Once Upon a Time in the West. Dir. Sergio Leone. Paramount Pictures, 1968.

Paris, Texas. Dir. Wim Wenders. Road Movies Filmproduktion, 1984.

The Passenger. Dir. Michelangelo Antonioni. Compagnia Cinematografica Champion, 1975.

Perfume: The Story of a Murderer. Dir. Tom Tykwer. Constantin Film Produktion, 2006.

The Piano. Dir. Jane Campion. CiBy 2000, 1993.

The Proposition. Dir. John Hillcoat. UK Film Council, 2005.

Pulp Fiction. Dir. Quentin Tarantino. A Band Apart, 1994.

Raiders of the Lost Ark. Dir. Steven Spielberg. Paramount Pictures, 1981.

Raise the Red Lantern. Dir. Yimou Zhang. Century Communications, 1991.

Ratcatcher. Dir. Lynne Ramsay. Pathé Pictures International, 1999.

Reconstruction. Dir. Christoffer Boe. HR. Boe & Co., 2003.

Requiem for a Dream. Dir. Darren Aronofsky. Artisan Entertainment, 2000.

Reservoir Dogs. Dir. Quentin Tarantino. Live Entertainment, 1992.

The Rock. Dir. Michael Bay. Don Simpson/Jerry Bruckheimer Films, 1996.

Rocky. Dir. John G. Avildsen. United Artists, 1976.

Rope. Dir. Alfred Hitchcock. Warner Bros. Pictures, 1948.

The Royal Tenenbaums. Dir. Wes Anderson. Touchstone Pictures, 2001.

Russian Ark. Dir. Aleksandr Sokurov. The Hermitage Bridge Studio, 2002.

The Secret in Their Eyes. Dir. Juan José Campanella. Tornasol Films, 2009.

Seopyeonje. Dir. Kwon-taek Im. Taehung Pictures, 1993.

Sex and Lucia. Dir. Julio Medem. Alicia Produce, 2001.

The Shawshank Redemption. Dir. Frank Darabont. Castle Rock Entertainment, 1994.

The Shining. Dir. Stanley Kubrick. Warner Bros. Pictures, 1980.

Sid and Nancy. Dir. Alex Cox. Zenith Entertainment, 1986.

The Silence of the Lambs. Dir. Jonathan Demme. Orion Pictures Corporation, 1991.

Solaris. Dir. Steven Soderbergh. Twentieth Century Fox Film Corporation, 2002.

The Soloist. Dir. Joe Wright. DreamWorks SKG, 2009.

Star Wars. Dir. George Lucas. Lucasfilm, 1977.

Taking Lives. Dir. D.J. Caruso. Warner Bros. Pictures, 2004.

Thelma & Louise. Dir. Ridley Scott. Metro-Goldwyn-Mayer, 1991.

The Thin Red Line. Dir. Terrence Malick. Phoenix Pictures, 1998.

Touch of Evil. Dir. Orson Welles. Universal International Pictures, 1958.

Trainspotting. Dir. Danny Boyle. Channel Four Films, 1996.

The Truman Show. Dir. Peter Weir. Paramount Pictures, 1998.

The Untouchables. Dir. Brian De Palma. Paramount Pictures, 1987.

Vertigo. Dir. Alfred Hitchcock. Paramount Pictures, 1958.

WALL·E. Dir. Andrew Stanton. Pixar Animation Studios, 2008.

What Time Is It There? Dir. Ming-liang Tsai. Arena Films, 2001.

Wings of Desire. Dir. Wim Wenders. Road Movies Filmproduktion, 1987.

index